SPEYSIDE RAILWAYS

SPEYSIDE RAILWAYS

exploring the remains of the
Great North of Scotland Railway
and its environs

Rosemary Burgess and Robert Kinghorn

ABERDEEN UNIVERSITY PRESS

First published 1988
Aberdeen University Press
A member of the Pergamon Group

© Rosemary A Burgess and Robert R F Kinghorn

British Library Cataloguing in Publication Data

Burgess, Rosemary
    Speyside railways: exploring the remains
    of the Great North of Scotland Railway
    and its environs.
    1. Scotland. Grampian Region. Railway
    Services. Disused Routes
    I. Title II. Kinghorn, Robert
    385′ .094121

    ISBN 0 08 036411 X

Printed in Great Britain
The University Press
Aberdeen

Contents

Illustrations

Abbreviations

LOS	= Lens of Sutton
RP	= Real Photographs
JLS	= J L Stevenson
KF	= Keith Fenwick
MDL	= Morayshire District Library
BR	= British Railways
HAV	= H A Vallance
AS	= A Sangster
BHC	= Barclay-Harvey Collection
RRFK	= R R F Kinghorn

Maps

Acknowledgements

We would like to thank all those who have helped us prepare this book. This especially includes all those who have let us use their copyrighted photographs; the Great North of Scotland Railway Association for allowing us to use their collection of photographs, and for the information provided in their Journal and by their members. All maps are by James Renny.

GNSR Class T no. 99, LNER class D41, as BR no. 62243. Courtesy Real Photograph Co.

I

Introduction

General

The object of this book is to describe the state of the railway lines
and stations along the valleys of the Rivers Spey, Fiddich and Isla, as
they were and as they are now, how they came to be there, how to
find what is left and what else of interest there is near each locality
(Map 1).

The majority of the lines were owned by the Great North of
Scotland Railway (GNSR) and a few by the Highland Railway (HR).
After the quarter century from 1923, as parts of the London & North
Eastern Railway (LNER) and the London, Midland & Scottish
Railway (LMSR) respectively, they were for less than twenty years in
the ownership of British Railways before being closed and having
most of their structures demolished. Once the track and other
movable fittings had been removed, the buildings, embankments,
bridges, etc. were, in general, left to their fate, although some bridges
carrying the line over rivers and roads were dismantled at the time of
the original closure. The state of what remains, after initial
dismantling, varies greatly. Some things have totally disappeared—
either by subsequent demolition or being engulfed by nature
reclaiming her own—while others are as good as new and still in use,
albeit for other purposes and without tracks.

Part of the track beds of two of these lifted lines have been
opened as the Strathspey Way. These are Ballindalloch to
Craigellachie and on to Dufftown and are a very pleasant means of
seeing this part of Scotland on foot, with exceptionally good views of
the rivers Spey and Fiddich. However, this book has been written
with the car driver, cyclist and road user as well as the walker in mind
and, where there is a choice, the directions are given for those
following the trackbed or visiting the stations by road. Where there is
no alternative only the road instructions are given. All map references
are to the metric 1 to 50,000 series Ordnance Survey maps. All

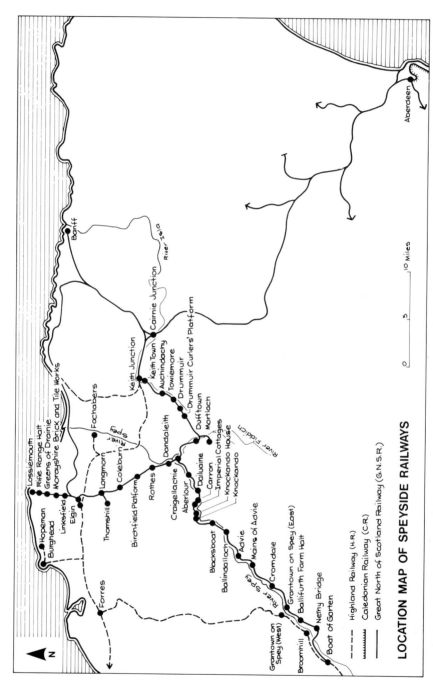

LOCATION MAP OF SPEYSIDE RAILWAYS

- - - - -   Highland Railway (H.R.)
·········   Caledonian Railway (C.R.)
─────   Great North of Scotland Railway (G.N.S.R.)

Map 1 General Map of the Railways of North East Scotland

distances are in miles and chains (80 chains = 1 mile) from Craigellachie and are based upon railway mileages. In addition to the railway we have tried to mention some of the other things of interest or beauty which can be seen in the neighbourhood, including the wild flowers now inhabiting the places where trains once ran. However, we would recommend that the facilities of the tourist boards are used: these bodies produce an excellent range of leaflets detailing all that is to be seen in each locality. They also provide a very good accommodation guide with photographs and telephone numbers which can remove many of the worries of where to spend each night.

Apart from those parts converted into the Speyside Way the remainder of the land is private and many of the station buildings are houses. Always obtain permission before entering on someone else's land; never damage their property or the wildlife; keep dogs under control; leave no litter and always close gates behind you.

The three lines to be described, Craigellachie to Elgin, Keith and Boat of Garten, form a rough Y, tilted slightly to the south west with Craigellachie at the centre and the other three towns at the extremities (Map 1). For the sake of convenience the lines will be described as those three separate sections, with the nearby ex-Highland Railway stations included for extra interest. This split is purely artificial as that is not how they were built or how, once they were all absorbed into the GNSR, the lines were operated.

Outline of Railway History of the Area

The principal lines described were built by three individual companies, albeit with the backing of the GNSR, from Dufftown to Keith, from Dufftown to Abernethy (via Craigellachie) and from Craigellachie to Elgin and Lossiemouth. Once they were all completed the line from Keith to Elgin was operated as part of the GNSR main line whilst the Speyside line was a branch.

The first railway proposals in North East Scotland were in 1844 for a line to link Inverness with Aberdeen, together with branches to Portsoy, Banff and Peterhead. Parliamentary powers were obtained but various financial crises delayed the construction so that on the direct route from Aberdeen to Inverness the GNSR owned only as far as Keith. The remainder of the route to Inverness was owned and operated by the GNSR's great rival, the Highland Railway. This had grown out of a local line (variously and chronologically the Inverness & Nairn, the Inverness & Elgin Junction and the Inverness and

1 Longmorn station building from rear, August 1986 (RRFK)

2 Dufftown station building from platform side, August 1986 (RRFK)

3 Longmorn waiting shelter, August 1986 (RRFK)

4 Craigellachie signal box. Courtesy Real Photograph Co.

5   Longmorn station house August, 1986 (RRFK)

6   GNSR footbridge at Rothes, 1935 (HAV)

Aberdeen Junctions Railways) and was eventually to stretch from near Perth to Thurso and from Keith to Kyle of Lochalsh. Whilst the GNSR had been engaged in its building other local lines had been promoted, namely the Morayshire, the Strathspey and the Banffshire Railways. The GNSR was alway looking for ways to bypass the Highland and get its own access to Inverness or, at the least, increase its proportion of the mileage between the two cities. the GNSR therefore encouraged these local lines and eventually amalgamated with them. The furthest west that the GNSR ever reached was Elgin and that was by two circuitous routes. One was by the Coast line from Cairnie Junction via Buckie and the other, the object of part of this book, was from Keith via Craigellachie (Map 1).

Dates for opening and closing are given in the historical summaries at the beginning of each chapter and apply to all stations on that part of the line unless specifically mentioned in the text.

Typical GNSR lineside features

All railways have their own styles of building and the GNSR was no exception. There is much to be seen of several styles used by the GNSR for its more permanent structures, e.g. stations and bridges. However, the smaller items such as signals and foot bridges have gone.

Much of the GNSR was single track with passing places. These were often at stations so that two platforms were provided. Where there was no passing place only a single platform was needed. The two-platform stations normally had the major building on the Elgin-bound side on the mainline and on the Boat of Garten side on the Speyside line. With the exception of Elgin none of the GNSR stations was large.

The main building often consisted of a wooden or stone edifice containing the ticket office, waiting and ladies rooms. Longmorn is a typical wooden station (1). Note the lean-to Gents at the left of the building and that there is no passenger entrance at the rear of the building, access presumably being via the platform (108), Knockando is another wooden station but this time with a conventional entrance from the road (51).

Stone stations are more common and normally had a glazed and wooden central façade to the platform, e.g. Dufftown (2). These had the station name in gold lettering on the glass panel above the centre doors. The internal layout is very simple with booking hall in the centre, ticket office and waiting room on either side (see plan of Auchindachy).

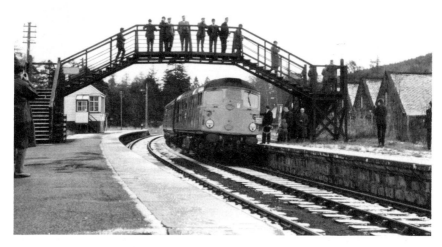

7   LNER footbridge at Carron, November 1968 (KF)

8   GNSR station name board at Nethybridge, August 1986 (RRFK)

9 Station seat at Keith Junction, August 1986 (RRFK)

10 Station weighbridge at Aberlour, August 1986 (RRFK)

On the opposite platforms were small wooden waiting shelters, although the only one which seems to have survived is that at Longmorn (3).

Another important building on a railway is the signal box or cabin. Again none of those on the lines visited has survived although we can see what Craigellachie box was like (4). It seems to have been of a wooden construction to match the buildings at Craigellachie or Longmorn. Only the base of this still exists and provides a viewing platform for the River Fiddich.

The railway staff had to live near the station and small houses were provided. Many on the GNSR were single storey L shaped buildings as at Longmorn (5). Other similar ones include the excise house at Coleburn, the much altered house at Birchfield Platform and Nethybridge. Some stations had two storey houses, e.g. Cromdale (63) and Nethybridge.

Where there were two platforms a footbridge was provided. The GNSR type was wooden, but all have long since gone (6). The LNER replaced these, but even their version has not stood the test of time and BR demolition teams. Carron in its later days had one of the LNER design (7).

Station name boards on the GNSR were four horizontal wooden planks with a moulded surround mounted on concrete posts. The station name was in large raised letters. Several survive, albeit without the letters, e.g. Nethybridge (8).

Other station impedimenta includes station seats, e.g. at Keith Junction (9) and weighbridges, e.g. at Aberlour (10). The GNSR lit its stations by oil lamps placed into brackets. Two types are to be seen, the free standing on top of a wooden pole as at Longmorn (11) or those attached to buildings, e.g. at Nethybridge (12). Mile posts with the mileage from Aberdeen in figures and dots for the quarters were placed every quarter mile and many are still to be seen, e.g. at Blacksboat (13). As with the signal boxes all the signals have been removed but many of the bases which supported the lattice work signal posts are to be found. That, east of Craigellachie, is where the trackbed is closed as the Speyside Way takes a small diversion (14).

The railway was fenced throughout its length, often with wire between wooden posts although sometimes round cast iron ones, marked 'Harper & Co. Abdn', were used (15). Access across the line for pedestrians was by kissing gates. Larger versions of these iron columns supported gates across roadways, as at Nethybridge (16).

The railway used a variety of bridges to cross and be crossed. The least common was the brick viaduct which crosses the Fiddich south of Dufftown (map reference 409329; 17). The more normal GNSR

11   GNSR freestanding lamp bracket at Longmorn, August 1986 (RRFK)

12 GNSR lamp bracket for a building at Nethybridge, August 1986 (RRFK)

practice was the girder bridge on stone pillars. Some of these had deep steel girders as at Craigellachie (18) whilst others had shallow girders as seen between Keith Town and Junction stations (19). The stone pillars also varied in their dimensions and number. Where the line is no longer in use the bridges have been removed, e.g. north of Cromdale (20). Where this has occurred on the Speyside Way replacement wooden structures (e.g. south of Carron) or suspension bridges (south of Aberlour) have been installed. The only exceptions are the two bridges on the Dufftown branch of the Way, one just south of Craigellachie station and the other halfway at Newton Bridge which carried the line high over the Fiddich (21). Smaller burns are crossed by more petite versions as at Towiemore (22 and 23). Minor roads crossed the railway by way of stone and steel bridges (24).

Lastly, the GNSR was famous for its great bridges crossing various rivers, notably the Spey. Two of these are encountered on these lines. The first, at Carron (40), is a steel lattice-work arch on stone pillars whilst the other, at Ballindalloch (55), is a box-girder bridge. Similar viaducts to that at Ballindalloch crossed the Spey between Nethybridge and the junction with the Highland Railway and between Dandaleith and Craigellachie on the main line to Elgin.

Elgin was the only station to have elaborate glass canopies over the platform (25); those over the terminus platforms at the east of the station have been removed.

Flora and Fauna

Disused railways often become a haven for wild flowers, animals and birds; depending on the time of year of your visit, you should find plenty of each. At all times, respect the Country Code. Do not disturb wildlife and never pick or uproot the plants.

The railways described pass through a variety of different habitats, all of which have distinctive vegetation.

Meadowland

This type of habitat, typically displayed near Aberlour and Cromdale, supports an abundance of wild flowers, seen at their best in summer, when at least fifty varieties can readily be found. From tiny common violets and speedwell to tall foxgloves, rosebay willow herb (fireweed) and meadowsweet. The Scottish thistle and harebell are also abundant.

Riverside

For most of the route, these railways run close to a river—be it Spey, Fiddich or Isla—and many marsh and water plants can be found. Where there is easy access to the banks of the Spey, such as north of Aberlour, by Knockando and Carron (see text), one finds water crowfoot tailing in the water and bright blue chicory on the banks. The red and yellow monkey-wort is another distinctive plant. Yellow iris (flags) and festoons of yellow honeysuckle can also be found adorning the banks.

Cuttings and Woodland

In the patches of woodland can be found both deciduous and coniferous trees—the most noticeable areas being on the part of the line out of Craigellachie towards Dufftown, and in the woodlands of Knockando. Where there are rock faces, stone abutments or in the Taminurie tunnel small plants and ferns cling. In sheltered places will be found wood avens, evening primrose (common mullein) and even spotted orchids, as well as abundant wild strawberries.

Station Sites

The fourth distinctive habitat which can be found is that around station buildings, many of which obviously had carefully tended gardens, now gone wild. Behind the station-master's house at Cromdale are vivid purple irises, with ox-eye daisies, canterbury bells and lupins, and from his fruit garden one could harvest raspberries, red and black currants and rhubarb. Ballindalloch is another good example of this with burnet and dog roses, with plenty of lupins and sweet peas reverting to the wild. Beyond Carron, near the site of the Imperial Cottages Halt, there is evidence of cultivation with forget-me-nots, indian balsam and an enormous bank of honeysuckle.

Wildlife

The Spey valley is well known for its wildlife, much of which attracts the sportsman, who is especially interested in salmon and roe-deer. The visitor should see plenty of rabbits and large hares in the meadows, and the flowers attract many species of butterfly, including

13 Milepost at Blacksboat, August 1986 (RRFK)

14 Base of signal post near Craigellachie, August 1986 (RRFK)

15   GNSR kissing gates near Knockando House platform, August 1986

16   GNSR station gates at Nethybridge, August 1986 (RRFK)

17   GNSR brick viaduct south of Dufftown, August 1986 (RRFK)

18   GNSR steel viaduct near Craigellachie carrying the Dufftown spur of the
Speyside walk, August 1986 (RRFK)

tortoiseshell and painted ladies. Kestrels and sparrowhawks can be seen hunting for prey along the valley. Curlews, pheasants and many other birds inhabit the area. Nearby, Loch Garten is famous for osprey. Woodpeckers may be found in the tree-lined parts of the line.

Scotch Whisky

A comparison of a location map of whisky distilleries and the railways covered in this book would show a marked correlation. That is no coincidence as most of the distilleries in the area came after the railway. The Spey and its tributaries provided the water of the required quality while the railway provided the transport for the inward coal and grain and the outward whisky.

Whisky is an anglicisation of the Gaelic 'uisge beatha' meaning water of life.

Malt whisky is made by a four-stage process: malting, mashing, fermentation and distillation. In the malting the barley is soaked in water for two to three days and then spread on a concrete floor to germinate. At this stage the starch becomes soluble. After eight to ten days the germination is stopped by drying the malted barley in the malt kiln. The kilns are heated by peat-fuelled fires and the smoke imparts a distinctive aroma. In the mashing stage the dried malt is ground and the resulting grist is mixed with hot water in the mash tun. The soluble starch is converted into a sugary liquid known as wort. This is separated and the remaining solids used as cattle food. Fermentation is when the wort is cooled and the sugar turned to alcohol by the action of yeast. This takes about 48 hours to produce a weak solution with unwanted impurities. Lastly comes distillation. The wash is twice distilled in large copper pot stills. The first still produces 'low wines' which, upon redistillation, become the final product.

Grain whisky differs in several ways. Malted barley is mixed with unmalted cereals which have been cooked in a steam pressure cooker, the wort is of a lower specific gravity, distillation is in a Coffey still and the final distillate of a higher strength.

Both malt and grain whiskies are left to mature in casks made of oak, often old sherry casks. The law says that this shall be for at least three years but many malts are left for fifteen to twenty-one years. After maturation the whisky is blended and reduced to the required strength by the addition of soft water. The water is often coloured and flavoured by the peat through which it has run. Thus the water is vital to a distillery and will decide its location. Some blends contain

19   GNSR steel viaduct between Keith Town and Keith Junction, August
1986 (RRFK)

20   Piers of dismantled viaduct north of Cromdale, August 1986

21   Piers of Newton Bridge between Craigellachie and Dufftown, August
1986 (RRFK)

22   Small GNSR steel bridge over burn south of Towiemore, August 1986
(RRFK)

23   Railside view of bridge, August 1986 (RRFK)

24   GNSR overbridge near Auchindachy, August 1986 (RRFK)

between fifteen and fifty different single whiskies. However, a considerable quantity of whisky is sold as single malt which has not been blended.

The basic definition of whisky is incorporated in law, normally the Finance Act because of the duty paid on it. The term 'Scotch' means that it has been distilled and matured in Scotland. Likewise Irish Whiskey has been distilled and matured in Ireland. Bourbon Whiskey is made from a mash of not less than 51 per cent corn grain and must be produced in the USA whereas Rye Whiskey must be produced from a mash of not less than 51 per cent rye grain.

The oldest reference to whisky in Scotland is in the Scottish Exchequer rolls for 1494. In 1644 the Scots Parliament passed an Excise Act fixing the duty at 2s. 8d per pint. The Scottish and English Crowns were united in 1603 and in 1707 the Act of Union united the Parliaments. However, that Act did not abolish the frontier so far as 'Colonial Liquors' which included Scotch Whisky, were concerned. Thus when the North British Railway started to run trains into England in 1846 there were delays as the customs men searched the luggage. Until the law was changed the NBR posted notices warning travellers not to take whisky into England.

25   Canopies at Elgin GNSR station, August 1986 (RRFK)

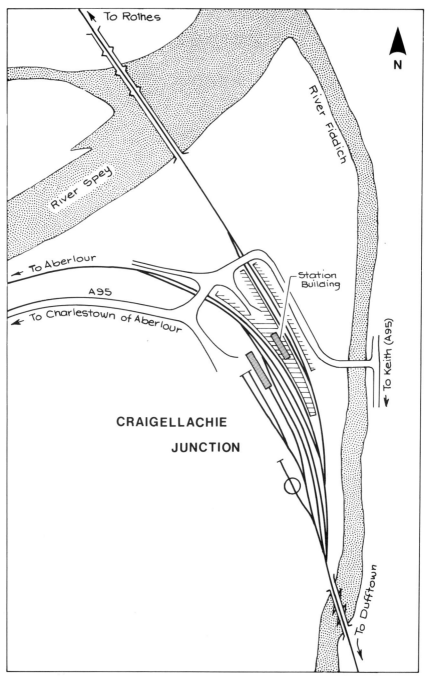

To Rothes

N

River Fiddich

River Spey

To Aberlour

A95

To Charlestown of Aberlour

Station Building

To Keith (A95)

CRAIGELLACHIE

JUNCTION

To Dufftown

Map 2 Craigellachie

II

Craigellachie

Because this station is being used as the centre of our descriptions, and thus occurs in each route, we shall examine it first of all.

Craigellachie station (293452, OS sheet 28, Elgin) is located to the north east of the town on the A95, towards Keith. The bridges where this road crosses the old line are clearly visible and the entrance to the station site is on the right between the bridge across the Speyside line and that over the mainline. It now looks like a large lay-by and is fenced off. This was the main entrance and led down to an island platform which had the northbound mainline (Elgin bound) on the left and Speyside branch platform on the right. There were substantial wooden buildings, now all gone, and a footbridge to the Keith and Aberdeen platform. The best access is now via the entry to Fiddich Park which is the original entrance to the goods yard and is on the Craigellachie side of the two bridges. Fiddich Park is the centre of the Speyside Way, which is also Y shaped. Two arms follow the dismantled railway lines, to Ballindalloch and Dufftown but the third follows a non-railway route to Spey Bay.

Opened on 1 July 1863, Craigellachie was called Strathspey Junction until 1 June 1865. It used to be an important junction with three platforms (Map 2; 26), but a comparison of photographs 27 and 28 with 29, 30 and 31 show that most of the station has disappeared. The station closed on either 6 May 1968 or 4 November 1968 according to different sources. The site is a centre of the Speyside Way and there is a car park, next to the remains of the Speyside branch platform, loos and an information centre with a map of the walks. The westerly ends of the platforms can be discerned under the undergrowth but all the buildings have long since gone. The platforms have been cut short and heavily planted with silver birch and other trees, as has the trackbed between the mainline platforms. It is impossible to follow the former mainline to the site of the bridge over the Spey because of the closeness of the planting of these trees. The Speyside trackbed and the goods yard are now the car park. At the north west end of the station the base of the signal box

26 Craigellachie shewing line from Dufftown crossing the Fiddich in the
foreground and bridge over the Spey to Elgin. The Speyside line curves
behind the hill to the left (LOS)

27 Craigellachie Speyside platform looking towards Dufftown.
Courtesy Real Photograph Co.

28 Speyside train at Craigellachie, May 1923 (BHC)

29 Craigellachie Speyside platform looking towards Dufftown, August 1986
(RRFK)

30 Craigellachie in LNER days. Elgin platform looking towards Dufftown
showing the signal box which overlooks the Fiddich (LOS)

31 Craigellachie Speyside platform, August 1986, taken from road bridge
(RRFK)

is now a viewing point for the River Fiddich (Map 2; 26) whilst the turntable has been filled in and a children's play area built in the circle. It has an excellent two-storey wooden play house with steps up and two slides down.

Craigellachie is a pleasant small town, built in terraces, in a very picturesque part of the Spey Valley at the confluence of the rivers Spey and Fiddich. It makes an ideal centre for these expeditions, having a few shops, post office, three hotels and several B & Bs. It is Victorian in character since its greatest period of growth occurred in the last quarter of the nineteenth century when its population quintupled. Early closing day is Thursday. It has a distillery and two cooperages. Just outside the town is Craigellachie Bridge, one of Thomas Telford's most elegant, which was built in 1814 at a cost of £8,000 (32). Its single cast-iron span of 150 feet was prefabricated at Plas Kynaston in Wales and is supported on castellated granite towers. Since 1964 it has been by-passed and good views of it can be obtained from the new but less elegant road bridge.

32   Telford's Craigellachie Bridge, August 1986 (RRFK)

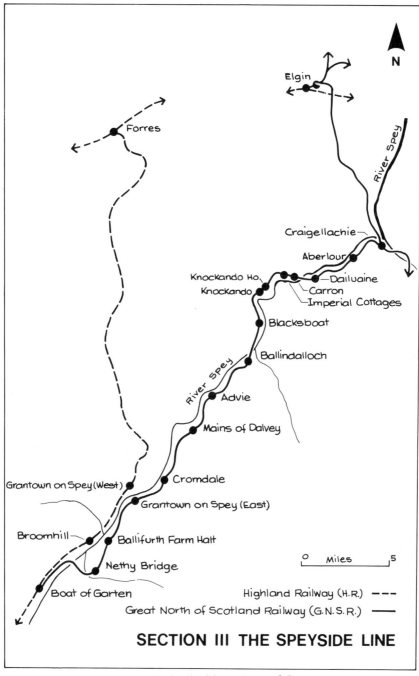

Map 3 Craigellachie to Boat of Garten

III

Craigellachie to Boat of Garten

History of the section

This $33\frac{1}{4}$ mile section (Map 3) was built by the Strathspey Railway who obtained their Act for the Dufftown to Craigellachie section on 14 July 1857 and for the remainder on 17 May 1861. The section from Dufftown to Abernethy (Nethy Bridge from December 1867) was opened on 1 July 1863. In 1866 the GNSR obtained an Act to build from Nethy Bridge to Boat of Garten and this line was opened on 1 August 1866. The junction was two miles north of Boat of Garten and one and a quarter miles south of Broomhill (HR) station. Traffic on the Highland line did not justify a signal box at the junction and the GNSR refused to contribute to its cost. Eventually, after a short interruption to through traffic, an extra track was laid by the HR for the sole use of GNSR trains. Thus, the two miles from the convergence of the GNSR with the HR to Boat of Garten were double track, actually two single lines running side by side, the physical junction being at Boat of Garten. Racing between trains of the two companies along this section was not unknown.

There were heavy engineering works on both the Fiddich and Speyside sections. The Fiddich is crossed near Dufftown by a bridge of two arches of 60 feet and is preceded by a very sharp curve (see Section IV). The Spey is fast flowing and drops about 13 feet per mile. Thus it has carved out a narrow twisting steep-sided gorge for itself alongside which the Strathspey railway had to be laid. Several tunnels were planned between Craigellachie and Blacksboat but these were opened out into cuttings before the line opened. In addition there were substantial wrought-iron bridges across the Spey at Carron and Ballindalloch, as well as a viaduct across the Alderdar Burn near Blacksboat, with numerous heavy stone bridges and culverts where minor burns and rivers flow into the Spey.

Passenger traffic was slow to develop and much of the freight on this line was traffic to and from the distilleries which line the bank of the Spey, especially between Cromdale and Carron. Now all that traffic uses the narrow local roads.

In 1884 there were three mixed trains a day each way with journey times between Craigellachie and Boat of Garten of about one and a half and two hours. By 1902 that had changed to two passenger, three mixed and two goods trains each way every day. In 1931 the timetable was for three passenger, one mixed and two goods each way. By the 1960s it was obvious that BR was trying to close the line. Connections with the mainline at Craigellachie were worsened so that a journey to Elgin or Aberdeen was impractical by rail. This just encouraged the switch to the use of private cars. On the freight side, individual wagon loads were discouraged and since distilleries could not justify a weekly block train of coal, grain or whisky the service was ended. The line was closed to passengers on 18 October 1965 and to freight in 15 November 1971. No doubt, as in other parts of Britain, the railway authorities would admit to having made a mistake. 'Marry in haste, repent at leisure': in the case of the railways replace the word 'marry' by 'close'.

The whisky industry was soon associated with the Speyside line. When first built the line did not serve any of the existing distilleries but some, such as those at Aberlour, Cromdale (Balmenach) and Carron (Dailuaine) used horses and carts for transport to the railway.

Cragganmore was the first distillery to open after the building of the line and was beside Ballindalloch station. Soon (by 1885) Dailuaine and Balmenach distilleries were connected by what were called 'tramways' with the Speyside line. Each had its own shunting engine and a network of sidings at the distillery.

The locomotive at Dailuaine distillery was a 0-4-0 saddle tank pug built by Andrew Barclay in 1939. Although there were exchange sidings at the junction this locomotive often worked trains to the station at Carron. The steam loco was kept in use by the distillery until the closure of the Speyside line, even after BR had dieselised the rest of the services.

At the junctions with the mainline, arrangements differed. Dailuaine had exchange sidings whereas Balmenach used the existing goods yard at Cromdale station.

In the late 1880s and 1890s there was a whisky distilling boom and on Speyside alone Tamdhu in 1896 (at Knockando), Imperial in 1897 (at Carron) and Knockando in 1899 (between Carron and Knockando) were built, complete with their own railway sidings. The first 'whisky special' ran in 1887 when 16,000 gallons of malt whisky were taken to Dundee.

The trackbed has been partly converted into the Speyside Way which is open as far south as Ballindalloch and affords magnificent views of some of the most scenic parts of the Spey. It was officially opened on Friday, 3 July 1981, although people had been using it for some time by then. Walking this section is a practical alternative to taking the car. However the part south of Ballindalloch has not yet been opened as a public right of way and road transport will be needed to visit that piece of the line.

The Speyside Way provides a good means of seeing part of the Spey valley. The walking is generally undemanding but the section from Craigellachie to Aberlour is especially easy.

Charlestown of Aberlour, 2m 31c (265430, OS sheet 28, Elgin)

If travelling by road leave Craigellachie on the A95 and Aberlour is the next village on the road. In the village, turn right immediately past the second church by the small park, and the station is fifty yards on.

If leaving Craigellachie on foot take the Speyside Way which follows the trackbed of the old Speyside line. The path goes under the road bridge and starts to swing sharply to the left to run along side the Spey (Map 2).

A short way along on the right is a flight of wooden steps down to the water's edge. If one descends these and then walks back along the bank some remains of the abutments which carried the mainline over the Spey to Elgin can be seen on thefar bank (33). The banks are overgrown by lush vegetation, in summer shrouded in yellow honeysuckle and gooseberries. Walking down to the shore, one can see long strands of water crowfoot with daisy-like white and yellow flowers in the water. The shingle at the edge of the river is littered with the shells of freshwater mussels.

Continuing along the Speyside Way a small culvert and bridge no. 503 are passed. Just after milepost 68¼ the Craigellachie bypass has obliterated the track but the Speyside Way is taken under it in a new pedestrian tunnel and quickly regains the old railway.

The track now passes into a small tree-lined cutting and heads for the sole tunnel on the line (structure no. 504) which is at Taminurie (34). The tunnel has stone portals but is without any retaining walls, the bare cliff being firm enough. On leaving the south end of this tunnel (35) the line crosses an iron girder bridge (no. 505) which leads to a rocky gorge for about 200 yards before views of the river are obtained once again. Immediately south of the tunnel and alongside the girder bridge is a massive brick retaining wall about 40 feet high

33   Abutment of Viaduct across the Spey on the Elgin side of the river
(RRFK)

34   Taminurie Tunnel from the north, August 1986 (RRFK)

35 Taminurie Tunnel from the south, August 1986 (RRFK)

and 100 yards long. This passes behind the bridge and along the gorge.

Small, rock-clinging plants are abundant here and tiny wild strawberries may be found. Many varieties of ferns can be found in and around the tunnel. The tunnel is surmounted by tall pine trees.

From here the walk to Aberlour is straighforward and many railway remains are to be seen. These include various bridges, e.g. no. 507 which has transverse wooden sleepers with iron railings across a small culvert, or no. 508 which has wooden decking on steel girders lain across between stone abutments. The fencing is mostly wire on wooden posts but look out for some of the circular cast-iron posts with the words 'Harper & Co., Abd.' on them. Track crossing gates (e.g. north of bridge 507) are to be seen, which employ these circular posts, in the form of kissing gates made with metal strips. All along this section one finds a wide selection of wild meadow flowers with some escapees from local gardens. The burnet rose rambles with blackberries over the smaller birds'-foot-trefoil, ladies' bedstraw, wood anemone, germander speedwell and many others.

A little north of Aberlour (Map 4) is an occupation crossing (by mp 69¾) with the tracks in place. Also to be seen are some remains of the ironwork on the sleepers associated with the points and signals at the approach to Aberlour station where the track bed widens (north of double track bridge no. 509). The goods shed is still on the left of the track and is made of corrugated iron, painted yellow with red roof and doors. The coal yard, also on the left, has a goods platform with the remains of a lampholder and a loading gauge.

From here the track has been obliterated to form the pleasant and well-tended Alice Littler Park in which the restored main station building now stands.

The principal station building (36 and 37) is in good condition, well maintained, rendered, pebble-dashed and painted white with

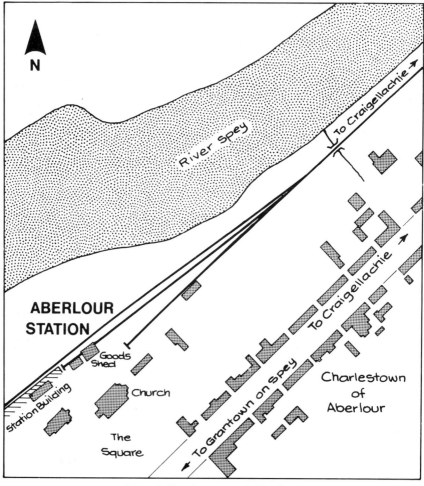

Map 4 Charlestown of Aberlour

36 Aberlour looking towards Craigellachie, November 1968 (KF)

37 Aberlour station, now a tearoom, August 1986 (RRFK)

unusual decorative mouldings over the door. It is now used as a tea-room by the ladies of the local kirk as a means of raising money. Very good homebaked teas and light meals can be obtained there for a reasonable amount and it makes a very welcome place to break one's journey, even if it has only just begun. In addition clean loos are available.

Only the south-bound platform with the station building survives, the other platform, waiting shelter and footbridge (no. 510), which was south of the station building, have been demolished to make way for gardens with well-kept lawns and flowerbeds which sweep down to the river. Steps of local stone lead from the platform to the lawn. The signal box (36), which was opposite the goods shed, has also disappeared. However, the goods shed (36) does survive in a nearby coal yard which has old railway gates on the road entrance.

On the north wall of the station is the old weighbridge made by Henry Pooley, while on the north east corner of the building is a GNSR lamp bracket which now contains an electric lamp. On the platform are old railway seats. Inside the tearoom are photographs of the station as it was in its halcyon days.

To the south of the station the track passes the station hotel (1896) and under a road bridge (no. 511). The path, lightly metalled with speed humps, divides after a short way. The right hand track, which is not the old railway, leads to a car park, children's play area and a suspension bridge across the Spey. This was built by the firm of James Abernethy & Co, engineers & builders of Aberdeen. It was provided by the local landowner to replace the ferry after a drowning accident. It is now owned by the Littlewoods family who charge a toll twice a year so as to retain control of it, otherwise it would become a public right of way. It has twin steel lattice pillars on each side which are set in concrete and have decorative ball and spike finials. Blue chicory, white water crowfoot and yellow monkey wort are among the colourful flowers at the water's edge. Look from the bridge to see the abundant water life.

The railway track and Speyside Way curves away to the left, past the cemetery and across the Lour burn. The old bridge (no. 512) had steel girders on stone abutments lain on the skew across the water, but this has been replaced by a very bouncy wooden suspension bridge.

The town of Aberlour, so named because it is situated close to the junction or mouth of the Lour with the Spey, lies between the Spey on one side and the Conval Hills and Ben Rinnes on the other. It was founded in 1812 by the local laird, Charles Grant of Wester Elchies. Locals say that the stones from the bed of the Spey were used to build the first houses.

Aberlour is a noted salmon fishing centre whilst the surrounding countryside is excellent for birdwatching. There are many riverside, woodland and hill walks starting from the village.

Besides two banks, Aberlour has a useful selection of shops and half-a-dozen varied eating places, restaurants, cafes, pubs and an attractive little square by the station.

The Aberlour-Glenlivet distillery has a visitors' centre with guided tours. The distillery is situated by the Lour burn which was once believed to require the sacrifice of a life at regular intervals. It is reputed that the distillery had a tradition of appeasing the river by offering it a measure of each new batch of whisky; after all, without the waters of the Lour there would be no whisky. It is said that it is no coincidence that the man who discontinued that practice met an early end while fishing from a boat. Also situated in Aberlour is the bakery where Walkers world famous shortbreads are produced, but the factory is not open to visitors.

Not far away is Archiestown on the B9102. It takes its name from Sir Archibald Grant of Monymusk who founded the village on the Moor of Ballintomb in about 1760. Close to Archiestown is the Ladycroft Farm Museum.

Either continue along the A95 to the south or walk along the Speyside Way to Dailuaine Halt.

•

Dailuaine Halt 4m 57c (237413; OS sheet 28, Elgin)

Continue along the A95 until reaching Bridge of Derrybeg (245406), then turn right on to an unclassified road. A short way along on the left is the wide entrance of the Dailuaine distillery. Immediately ahead on the left of the road is the old siding to the distillery with a road overbridge (38). The track of the distillery branch can be followed to its junction with the mainline (about three quarters of a mile) which is just under the road overbridge at 230412. This bridge is skewed across the railway and has iron sheeting parapets. The siding was in use until 4 November 1971.

Just past the entrance to the distillery is a turning on the right which leads down a steep, poorly made road to Dailuaine Halt (39). When the road meets the old railway there is a bridge over a stream to the right but to the left the trackbed passes in front of a steep slope. Because of the high trees on the right of the line the impression of a steep cutting is obtained. A modern tubular steel gate crosses the line at this point. Dailuaine Halt is tucked in at the base of the slope on the left of the track. The platform is built of wooden sleepers and the old station nameboard is still there but recently repainted so as to obscure the name. This halt was opened in 1934 by the LNER.

Either return on the road to the distillery and turn right on to the unclassified road or continue walking along the track passing Dailuaine Distillery junction on the way. The section from Dailuaine to Carron was marshy and subject to landslides. Water has been known to come down the distillery branch and cross the mainline, depositing debris on the way.

Shortly after the skew bridge over the distillery siding, just by the junction of that branch with the main line, the mainline bridge over the road has been demolished but there is still a dog-leg in the road where it used to be. Walkers along the Speyside Way are advised to join the road here.

The road and the railway shared a major wrought iron bridge (40) over the Spey. Separating the two are cast iron panels bearing the inscription 'Mackinnon & Co. Engineers, Aberdeen, 1863'. In 1986 a vehicle badly damaged some of these panels and the structure of the bridge can more readily be seen (41).

Once over the Spey the track of the railway is very overgrown but, although the Speyside Way follows the road until after Carron

38   End of Dailuaine distillery branch looking towards junction, August 1986 (RRFK)

39 Dailuaine station looking towards Boat of Garten, August 1986 (RRFK)

40 Carron Bridge, August 1986, Boat of Garten to the left, Craigellachie to the right (RRFK)

Station it is possible to walk from the river to the station along the course of the line. The Spey here has steep, wooded banks, mostly of deciduous trees.

Carron 5m 59c (223412, OS sheet 28, Elgin)

A quarter of a mile past the river bridge, in the village of Carron, the major road turns right but the station (42 and 43) is to the left down a track which leads to the Imperial Distillery. The stone station buildings, platform and level crossing gates are all in place and belong to the distillery. The buildings have many original features including the clock, drinking fountain and central double doors (44). The trackbed has been grassed over and the station has become the entrance to the distillery with the station sign reversed on its uprights so that it faces the road rather than the platform. Between the unclassified road from the river bridge and the station is the site of the goods yard and the goods loading platform is clearly visible next to that road. The base of a long thin goods building can also be discerned.

A short distance along the platforms, in the direction of the river, trees have been planted between the platforms and on them: silver birch on the northbound and pine on the southbound (45). However, amongst these can still be seen a standard, but rather bent, GNSR lampholder and the station nameboard. Although the letters have been removed the name is still visible. This heavy afforestation of platforms and embankments, also seen at Craigellachie, makes walking very difficult, and is rapidly obscuring railway features. As in so many other places, the footbridge (42) has been removed.

Leave the station on the Speyside Way, which is now back on the old trackbed or drive along the lane which runs NW alongside the old line.

Imperial Distillery 6m 19c and Imperial Cottages Halt
(215416, OS sheet 28, Elgin)

The distillery had a private siding, opened in 1897, but there is no account of its closure. The Cottages Halt opened on 15 June 1959 and lasted until the end of passenger services on the whole line (18 October 1965). There are no obvious remains of this halt and it seems to have completely disappeared. However, its most likely location is just south of the cottages by what used to be a small level crossing. The trackbed passes through a mixture of woodland and farmland. The trackside is lined with flowers such as wood sorrel, rest harrow,

41 Detail of Carron Bridge shewing the damaged partition between the road and the railway sections of the bridge, August 1986 (RRFK)

42 Carron station in GNSR days looking towards Craigellachie (LOS)

43 Carron station, August 1986 looking towards Craigellachie. Station building on the right (RRFK)

44   Carron station building, August 1986 (RRFK)

45   Carron station looking towards Carron Bridge and Craigellachie (LOS)

46   Knockando House Halt looking towards Craigellachie, August 1986
(RRFK)

indian balsam, cinquefoil, St John's wort and a memorable honeysuckle bank near a farm entrance

Drivers return to Carron Station and take theunclassified road to Knockando. Take the left fork at the tee junction at 224423 and again at the B9102 (212437). At the crossroads at Caldow (194428) turn left to Knockando House, park the car at the end of the road andwalk.

Alternatively one may walk from Carron or from Knockando (both about one and a quarter miles).

Knockando House Platform 6m 78c (195415, OS sheet 28, Elgin)

This was opened in 1869 as Knockando. One and a quarter miles from Carron, it was a private platform serving the Knockando Estate. It was renamed Knockando House in 1905 when the next station down the line was renamed Knockando.

Where the path from Knockando House reaches the Speyside Way the platform is the site of the station (46). North of that point are typical GNSR round top posts and kissing gates (15). The platform is on the western side of the line immediately south of the path from the House. It is wooden, overgrown and built into the bank.

Along this section several bridges have been demolished and subsequently replaced for the Speyside Way. For instance, north of this station bridge no. 525 has been rebuilt in wood on the original massive stone pillars (47). This carries the Speyside Way high over a major tributary of the Spey, the Ballintomb Burn. The stone bridge over the road just north of this burn has had new steel handrails fitted. Likewise to the south of this station the track crosses a stream and an unmade road by a new bridge. This is labelled 'Bridge replaced by Rhine Troop, 54th. Squadron, Royal Engineers. May 13th 1980'. This part of the track isheavily wooded, and is a rewarding area for birdwatchers.

Either retrace one's route back to B9102 and turn left on to it or continue along the Strathspey Way.

Knockando Timber Siding 7m 59c (194415) and **Knockando Distillery** 7m 67c (196414, OS sheet 28, Elgin)

These were two private sidings opened in 1918 and on 16 October 1905 respectively. There is no account of their closure but no visible remains are evident.

47 Boat of Garten bound GNSR train near Knockando about 1910 (BR)

48 Gilbey's Cottage Halt looking towards Boat of Garten, August 1986
(RRFK)

Gilbey's Cottage Halt 8m 3c (194415, OS sheet 28, Elgin)

Access is best by walking along the Speyside Way.

This halt opened on 15 June 1959 and lasted until the end of passenger traffic on 18 October 1965. The location of the actual site is difficult to ascertain but it is probably at the back of Knockando distillery, which in 1904 had been bought by W A Gilbey. There are gate posts, the remains of a buffer stop and some track remains (48). This distillery produces J & B Special Rare, Mrs Thatcher's favourite tipple.

Knockando 8m 18c (192417, OS shcct 28, Elgin)

If travelling by road follow the B9102 for a quarter of a mile and turn very sharp right on to the road to Tamdhu Distillery (188437). Proceed down this road, passing a woollen mill and shop, and park outside the station buildings.

A distillery siding was open here by 29 May 1896, and the station was opened on 1 July 1899. Until 2October 1905 it was known as Dalbeallie, pronounced by the locals as Dal-bee-allie! (Map 5; 49, 50 and 51). The whole station except the tracks is extant and in very good condition. It is the visitors' centre for the Tamdhu Distillery, the home of The Famous Grouse Whisky. Because a rival establishment a little further along the river has the name Knockando the signs now proclaim this station as Tamdhu—its third name. Tamdhu is Gaelic for Black Tam.

The distillery was built in 1896 on a site selected for its proximity to both the railway and the pure waters of the Knockando Burn. However, for 21 years the production was interrupted because of problems with the disposal of the effluent and production recommenced in 1947. The visitors' centre is open 10am to 4pm, Mondays to Fridays, Easter to September.

The wooden station building, concrete store hut (used to store goods for the shop in the visitors' centre) and wooden signal box (complete with signal levers) are on one platform and a wooden waiting hut is on the other. All are painted white. In addition to information about the distillery the display in the exhibition room at the station contains some pictures and notices pertaining to the railway. There is also a small shop where souvenirs can be purchased. The distillery is to be praised for its imaginative use of this station and the way it has preserved the buildings. Besides being able to walk along the trackbed (part of the Speyside Way) and obtain good views of the rivervalley it is possible to descend to the river bank and see

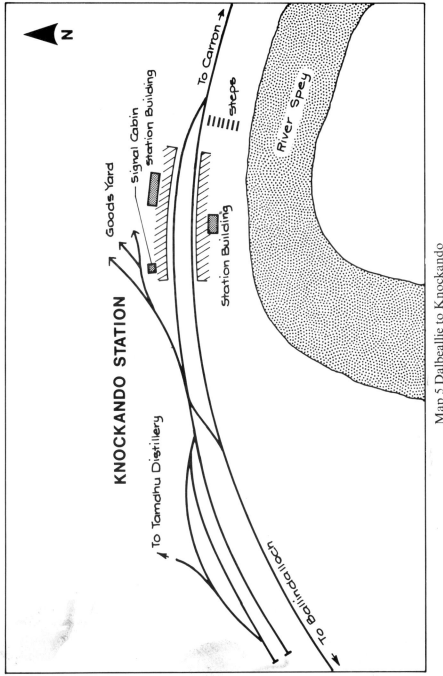

Map 5 Dalbeallie to Knockando

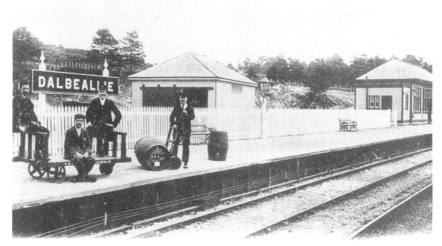

49   Dalbeallie station looking towards Craigellachie (MDL)

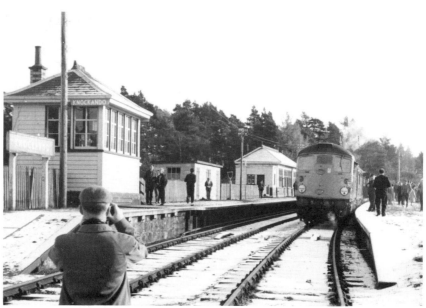

50   Knockando looking towards Craigellachie, November 1986 (KF)
1968

this mighty stream. The steps to the water's edge are just by the north end of the platforms, and it is well worth climbing down to see the torrent rushing past lichen covered rocks.

Either return to the B9102 and turn left or walk southwards along the Speyside Way.

Blacksboat 10m 36c (183389 OS sheet 28, Elgin)
Continue on the B9102 to the junction with the B9138 (181388), signposted to 'Marypark, 1m.'. As this road turns to cross the trackbed and the river the station is on the right.

The station got its name from the ferry boat which used to ply across the river, and the locals (and certainly one porter) pronounced it Bla-acksboat (Map 6; 52).

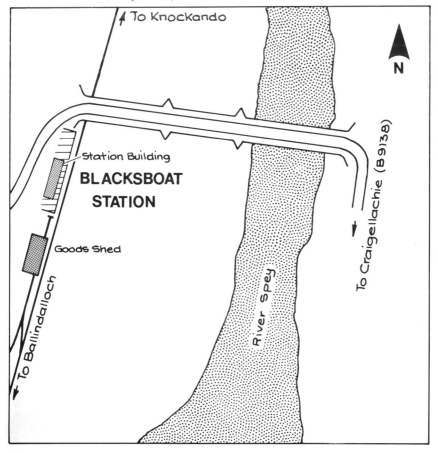

Map 6 Blacksboat

51   Tamdhu looking north, August 1986 (RRFK)

52   Blacksboat looking to Boat of Garten, June 1957 (JLS)

Both the station building and the goods shed remain. The station building is of stone and has been renovated in connection with the Speyside Way, Blacksboat being one of the recommended joining places. The wooden central section of the station is freshly painted black and white (53 and 54). The platform exists from the station building to the road overbridge.

The goods shed, slightly to the south of the station, is in use as a hay store. It is constructed of horizontal wooden boards painted cream with brown vertical boarded doors. Just south of the station is mp $78\frac{1}{4}$ in fairly good condition.

The river valley has opened out a little at this point and superb views are to be obtained from many vantage points in the area, especially acrossthe river. The road crosses three bridges as it traverses this wide part of the river valley. The first bridge, immediately after the steep descent from the B9102, is across the mainline. It consists of stone abutments with steel girders supporting the road, and steel sheeting sides. The second bridge is identical and much closer to the river as if there was a siding along to the water's edge. The third bridge is that over the river which replaced the ferry.

Near here the railway had to cross the Alderdar burn and a three span viaduct was employed. This had two spans of 40 feet and one of 50 feet and was 50 feet high being built on piles 15 feet long followed by 16 feet of masonry. All those supports are below the ground. Just south of this station is the deepest cutting on the whole GNSR system.

Either continue along the B9138, over the Spey towards the A95, or walk on south along the Speyside Way. Between Blacksboat and Ballindalloch the bridge over the river Geallaidh and several smaller streams have been replaced either by the standard Speyside Way suspension bridges or planks laid across between the old abutments.

Ballindalloch 12m 22c (166366, OS sheet 28, Elgin)

Turn right on the A95. As this road descends into the gorge of the River Avon there is a hairpin bend with the Danashaugh Inn on the corner. At this point is the B9008 to Tomintoul, one of the highest settlements in Great Britain and where panoramic views can be obtained. A little way further on theright, before the bridge over the Avon, is the entrance to Ballindalloch Castle. This has been the seat of the Macpherson-Grant family since 1546. It is sixteenth-century with later additions. It is only open on Sundays between 2pm and 4pm from May to September. J & G Grant's Glenfarclas distillery

53   Blacksboat, August 1969 (KF)

54   Blacksboat, August 1986 (RRFK)

and whisky museum are also nearby. Half a mile after the river crossing turn right on to the B9137 (177360) and proceed to the end of this road, about a mile.

Walking along the Speyside Way one has to cross the Spey once more by a major viaduct before reaching Ballindalloch station, the present temporary southern end of the Way. It is clearly marked with an information board. The section of the Way north of the viaduct passes through young pine forest, containing many game birds which are bred locally. The crossing of the Spey is achieved by a 198 foot-long lattice metalwork viaduct. It is built on brick pillars which carry it 20 feet clear of the normal water level. Makers plates at both ends have the legend: 'G. Macfarlane, Engineer, Dundee. 1863.' The bridge has been planked and provided with handrails for the convenience of walkers.

Flowers and shrubs border this path to the station as it passes between the goods yard and the river. Bushes of gorse, broom and wild roses overshadow the smaller flowers, and there are abundant clumps of rosebay willow herb, vetch and grasses. Around the goods yard and station many formerly cultivated plants are to be found, as mentioned inthe introduction. There are lupins of many colours, sweet peas as well as blackberries and raspberries. Views over the meadow to the riverbank offer opportunities to spot birds and wild animals—rabbits are particularly common.

On the left is the remains of an extensive goods yard and timber sidings which are between the railway and the B9137. The timber sidings had closed by 13 June 1930. Still existing is the wooden single-storey building with vertical wooden ribbing and a corrugated iron roof. It has a central brick chimney stack with two hexagonal chimney pots. There is also a second long goods shed with corrugated iron roof and the remains of a loading bay. On the opposite side of the road is a third wooden building together with about 160 numbered cattle pens.

The station (Map 7; 56 and 57) is just south of the end of the Speyside Way. The building is a brick edifice with red woodwork and the station name in foot high letters under the eaves. The house is in private use, possibly as some sort of hostel.

The two platforms are extant but heavily overgrown with young trees, gorse bushes and other plants. On the northbound platform some of the fencing has survived. Between the end of the Speyside Way and the platforms are the remains of the footbridge supports and a weighbridge made by Henry Pooley & Co Ltd, Birmingham & London.

Follow the B9137 back to the A95 and turn right.

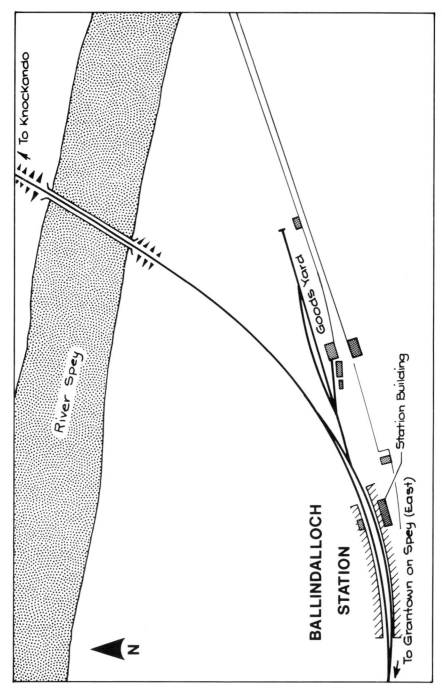

To Knockando

River Spey

Goods Yard

Station Building

BALLINDALLOCH STATION

To Grantown on Spey (East)

N

Map 7 Ballindalloch

55 Ballindalloch Viaduct looking towards Craigellachie, August 1986 (RRFK)

Advie 15m 30c (127347, OS sheet 28, Elgin)

The original Advie station was at map reference 136348 (14m 60c). It opened on 1 July 1863 and closed on 1 September 1868 when the new station was opened. To reach the site turn off the A95 at 136343 on to a track which leads to the disused trackbed. The old station was where the two meet.

To reach the later Advie station drive south on the A95 and turn right on to the unclassified road to Advie and Tulchan (122341). Where this road turns sharp left and then rises to cross a hump-backed bridge there is a house and shop on the right and an unmetalled track on the left marked 'To the Cemetery'. Follow this track and eventually it turns sharply right on to the trackbed, passing the platform. That is all that is left of a large station which boasted an ornate wooden building (58, 59 and 60). The platform site is heavily afforested with very little evidence of the old station building. There are some railway fence posts intact and a row of railway cottages on the west of the line.

This was the nearest station to Tulchan Lodge, a shooting lodge often frequented by the Prince of Wales, later King George V, which

56 Ballindalloch Station looking towards Craigellachie, August 1986
(RRFK)

57 Ballindalloch Station looking towards Craigellachie (HAV)

58   Advie looking towards Boat of Garten, June 1957 (JLS)

is why the station was so elaborate. Tulchan Lodge is still a hunting lodge with fishing and shooting available.

If one continues on the unclassified road the river is reached at a point where it is in a fairly wide plain and good views are obtainable. The Spey is crossed by a narrow ornamental concrete bridge.

Return to the A95 and turn right at the monument. For the next few miles the line is fairly visible from the road but some of the bridges over small burns are out and walking this section might be difficult.

Mains of Dalvey Halt 17m 50c (110322, OS sheet 36, Grantown & Cairngorm) (Sometimes spelt Dalvie)
Follow the A95 southwards until at the milestone at Mains of Dalvey, just before a wee burn crosses under the road to join the Spey.

The original Dalvey station (17m 40c) existed from 1 July 1863 to 1 September 1868. Dalvey Farm Halt or Mains of Dalvey Halt was opened by British Railways on 15 June 1959 and lasted until the closure of the whole line to passengers on 18 October 1965. Nothing remains of either halt, although the trackbed is clearly visible

59 Advie, August 1968 (KF)

60 Advie looking to Craigellachie, August 1986 (RRFK)

opposite Dalvey Farm (Mains of Dalvey on the OS map). The railway bridge over the stream by the farm is still intact and next to the road bridge. Along this section parts of the line have become lost recently due to road works.

Continue south on the A95.

Cromdale 21m 19c (072287, OS sheet 36, Grantown & Cairngorm)

Cromdale station is situated in a huge shallow basin. Heading south on the A95 note where a goods branch to the Balmnach Glenlivet distillery in the Haughs of Cromdale crossed under the road (074285) immediately after the river is crossed (61). This branch is 1 mile 40 chains long and was opened about 1885. Almost immediately after crossing over the track of this branch turn right at a crossroads on to an unclassified road to Mains of Cromdale (073284). The station is a quarter of a mile down this road on the right just before the hump-backed bridge over the trackbed.

The old station houses are by the road with the station building a little further on. South east of the station is a goods platform which was probably the headshunt for the line from the distillery which did not make a direct connection with the mainline. At this point there is extensive sleeper fencing.

The trackbed is readily accessible here and walkable for some way, especially to the south where one can walk under the road (bridge no. 570) on to the next bridge (no. 571) and beyond. The line curved gently to the left as it headed south from Cromdale station. To the north the line rises to cross a small stream and good views of the line to the distillery and the road bridges over that and the stream can be obtained from here (61). The bridge has been removed but was probably steel girders lain between stone abutments and across two stone pillars in standard GNSR fashion (20). The embankments are easily descendable and climbable and there are sufficient stepping stones in the water to allow one to cross the stream and walk to the north. North of this stream the line is on an embankment but soon passes into a shallow cutting.

The platforms are well defined and, unlike so many GNSR stations in the area, not planted with trees. The station building is a typical GNSR structure being stone built with a wooden central section to the platform side (62 and 63). The position of the clock is indicated by a circular mark on the stone and the date 9/11/56 on the station woodwork would infer that this was the last time it was redecorated. It is now heavily vandalised. On the opposite platform is the remains of the base of a waiting shelter.

61 A95 crossing the Cromdale to Balmenach Glenlivet distillery branch and
river, August 1986 (RRFK)

62   Cromdale looking towards Craigellachie, August 1986 (RRFK)

63 Cromdale looking towards Craigellachie (HAV)

64 Cromdale looking towards Boat of Garten, August 1986 (RRFK)

At right angles to the track are a station house and a cottage with a small wooden extension painted cream above green (64).

In the Haughs of Cromdale was fought the Battle of Cromdale (1690) which resulted in a heavy defeat for the Highlanders supporting James II.

In Cromdale is the Spey Valley Smokehouse which produces not only traditional smoked salmon but smoked trout, quail, pheasant, duck, turkey, goose, venison and lamb.

Return to the A95 and turn right.

Grantown-on-Spey East (GNSR) 24m 13c (039262, OS sheet 36, Grantown & Cairngorm)

Until 1 June 1912 the station was plain Grantown, the East suffix being added by British Railways.

Follow the A95 southwestwards to Grantown. The new A95 seems to be obliterating part of the trackbed west of Congash to the junction of the A95 with the Tomintoul road. The old A95 bridge over the GNSR at this junction (043262) looks as if it will be soon destroyed.

The new A95 will run south and east of Grantown East station, which should be clearly visible from the new road. The old A95 ran to the north of the station. To the west of the station the new road joins the old at what was the junction of the A95 and B970. (Old and new OS maps would be useful to explore this part.) The road underbridge at this point has been destroyed.

The station is best approached from the old A95. Entrance to the station site is by the row of dilapidated railway cottages. The station was the centre for the construction gangs building the new A95 but it will not be demolished by those works. Being clearly visible from the new road it would be an ideal site for some entrepreneur to convert it to a wayside cafe.

The platforms are intact but everything other than the station building has been levelled (65 and 66). The base of the footbridge is to be found, as is one GNSR kissing gate. The building is a standard GNSR stone and wood structure but in a poor state of repair. The roof looks weather-tight.

It is worth taking a diversion along the A95 to Grantown-on-Spey. This is a very pleasant town with many shops and eating places; it makes a good place to rest and refresh oneself. Not far away is Castle Grant, principal residence of the Grants of Grant, who caused this town to be built in 1765. It was considerably altered in the eighteenth century by John Adam. Also in Grantown are the few remains of the Highland station.

Grantown-on-Spey West (HR) (024270, OS sheet 36, Grantown & Cairngorm)

Follow the A95 through Grantown and shortly after the left hand turn into the town centre, take a side road on the right (027272).

The site of the station is now an industrial estate. Only the station master's house remains standing, all the station having been flattened. The platform edges are visible but the space in between them has been filled (67). The bases of a few lamp posts, cut off at the ground, and the base of a crane are also to be seen.

Return the way one has come along the A95 and take the B970 to Nethy Bridge.

Ballifurth Farm Halt 26m 53c (014236, OS sheet 36, Grantown & Cairngorm)

The halt was open from 15 June 1959 until the end of passenger services on 18 October 1965.

Turning right off the B970 at map reference 017234, the site of the halt was by the over bridge.

Return to the B970 and turn right.

Nethy Bridge 28m 61c (001208, OS sheet 36, Grantown & Cairngorm)

Turn right at the cross roads at the far end of the town. The station is on the right. Until December 1867 it was known as Abernethy.

The stone building (Map 8; 68 and 69), with its name in glass over the door, is now a private residence, possibly a hostel. From the road to a little way north of the station the trackbed is clear but after that it is overgrown with gorse and other shrubs, silver birch saplings and the inevitable rosebay willow herb—so much so that it is engulfing the platform and the notice board with the station name. There is a goods platform some way to the west of the station across what would have been the goods yard (71 and 72).

Standard GNSR gates are to be found by the road entrance to

65 Grantown East looking towards Boat of Garten, June 1958 (HAV)

66 Grantown East looking towards Boat of Garten, August 1986 (RRFK)

67 Grantown West (HR) looking towards Inverness, August 1986 (RRFK)

68 Nethybridge looking towards Craigellachie, November 1968 (KF)

69   Nethybridge Station, August 1986 (RRFK)

70   Level crossing south of Nethybridge Station, November 1968 (KF)

71 Level crossing south of Nethybridge, August 1986 (RRFK)

72 Broomhill (HR) looking to Inverness, August 1986 (RRFK)

both the goods yard and the station. The station and platforms have GNSR lampholders and the glass panel over the central doors has the name 'Nethy Bridge' on it. To the north east of the station is the station master's house. This is now private, but from the gate one can see a station seat beside the house. The level crossing gates are still there but the bridge over the stream on the other side of the road has been removed.

Nethy Bridge stands at the edge of the ancient Abernethy Forest of Caledonia, a remnant of the once vast pine forests which covered much of Scotland. Some 1,500 acres of the Forest near Loch Garten were purchased by the Royal Society for the Protection of Birds, chiefly because they contain the famous Osprey nesting site, but also

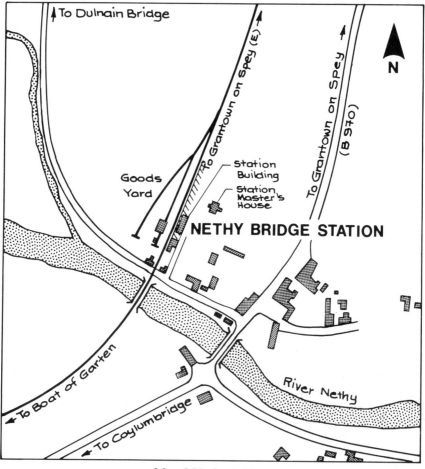

Map 8 Nethy Bridge

as this is a haven for many other birds including crested tits, Scottish crossbills, capercaillie, golden plover and many more. Nethy Bridge has some shops and a few hostelries; again a good place to break one's journey.

Leave by turning right on to the unclassified road and head towards the river.

Broomhill (HR) (994226 OS sheet 36, Grantown & Cairngorm)

Continue along this road and cross the Spey. Just after a sharp left hand turn the station is on the right.

The platform and trackbed are still there (72). The northern ramp of the platform is sleeper built. The station building has gone but on the opposite side of the line are two station cottages, one of which is occupied, and a house (73), also occupied and identical to that at Grantown West.

One can either continue along the unclassified road to join the A95 and turn left to drive to Boat of Garten. A good viewpoint of the piers of the GNSR viaduct across the Spey can be seen from map reference 986225. Alternatively return across the Spey and follow the B970 to Boat of Garten.

Boat of Garten 33m 41c (943189, OS sheet 36, Grantown & Cairngorm)

From the B970 there are several side roads where access to the old track may be obtained (Map references: 997205; 989208 and 984207). The latter is the nearest point to the site of the now demolished viaduct over the Spey.

Boat of Garten station was opened by the Highland Railway when it opened its mainline (via Forres and Grantown) from Inverness to Stanley Junction, north of Perth. It was the terminus of GNSR trains on their Speyside line, which used the outer face of the island platform. The actual convergence of the lines was two and a quarter miles north (978219). The nearest road access to the site is at Croftnven off the A95 (978225).

Boat of Garten (74, 75, 76 and 77) is now the headquarters of the new Strathspey Railway which operates steam trains, with refreshment facilities, to Aviemore (Speyside), whence connection can be made with ScotRail on the BR mainline to Inverness via Carrbridge. The Highland Railway opened this cut off between 1892 and 1898 to shorten its mainline to discourage other companies who

73   Station House Broomhill (HR), August 1986 (RRFK)

74 Boat of Garten in HR & GNSR days looking north (note old location of footbridge) (LOS)

75 Boat of Garten looking north, August 1986 with relocated footbridge (RRFK)

76 Boat of Garten station, August 1986 (RRFK)

were planning rival routes to Inverness, mostly via the Great Glen. These included the proposed Glasgow & North Western, The West Highland and the North British. In addition the Strathspey Railway have a museum, bookshop, loos and an interesting collection of engines (mostly post grouping and BR), coaches and wagons (from all periods).

The part timber, part stone station is fully restored and painted brown and cream. Besides the main building on the up platform there is a Highland footbridge (moved from its original position, see 74, 75 and 57) and a waiting shelter.

77   Boat of Garten looking north with Speyside train, June 1958 (HAV)

IV

Craigellachie to Keith

History of the section

The description of this section again begins at our centre point of Craigellachie.

This 13¾-mile line was built in two parts (Map 9). The Strathspey Railway obtained powers to build from Dufftown, through Craigellachie (Strathspey Junction until 1865) to Nethy Bridge on 17 May 1861 and the line opened on 1 July 1863. This was to join up with the Dufftown and Keith Railway whose Act is dated 27 July 1857 and which opened for goods on 19 February 1862 and for passengers two days later. The same dates as the Strathspey line was authorised and opened apply to the extension of the Morayshire Railway from Dandaleith (Craigellachie until 1865) to Craigellachie (Strathspey Junction until 1865). All these railways were protégés of the GNSR and from the opening of the Morayshire and the Strathspey lines the former, together with the Dufftown and Keith, was worked as a through mainline from Aberdeen to Elgin via Keith and Craigellachie and the latter was a branch.

When the line opened only three distilleries were served by the railway. Soon another seven were opened along the railway and the Mortlach branch opened to serve three others.

In June 1863 there were three mixed trains each way between Keith and Dufftown. When the line became a part of the GNSR mainline from Aberdeen to Elgin the service reflected this. In 1884 there was one passenger, three mixed and five goods trains per day. By 1902 the service was six passenger and seven goods per day, three of the passenger and two of the goods services being express. The service remained at this sort of level for the next sixty years, albeit with minor modifications, the Keith-Dufftown section requiring between 22 to 28 minutes. In the 1960s diesels were introduced and the line ceased to be a mainline so connections had to be made at

73

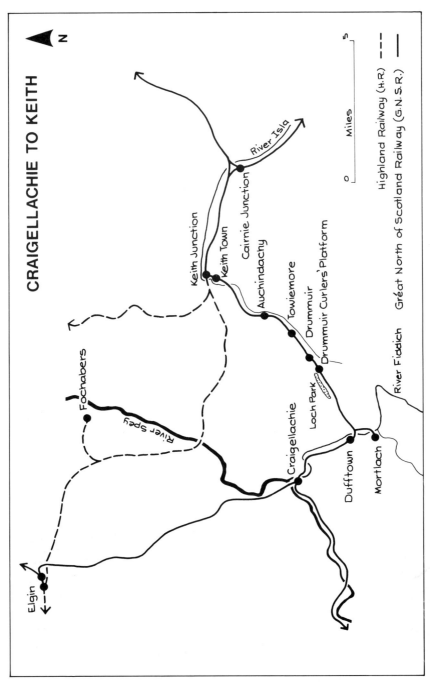

Map 9 Craigellachie to Keith Junction

Elgin and Keith. In addition to the extra time needed for the change of train, the actual journey times increased even though some stops were omitted. The incentive not to use the railway was maximised by the railway authorities.

The line from Craigellachie to Keith was closed to passengers from 6 May 1966 and after November 1971, with the exception of the section from Dufftown to Keith, was completely closed and lifted. Thus the earliest part to open, Keith to Dufftown, is the only section which sees any traffic, grain etc to the various distilleries in Dufftown and the twice-weekly, summer only, *Northern Belle* which brings tourists to the Glenfiddich distillery or to Drummuir House.

The only section with heavy engineering works is along the gorge of the Fiddich. Here the river follows a twisting path through its valley and between Craigellachie and Dufftown the line crossed the river twice. Once just south of Craigellachie and again half way to Dufftown at Newton Bridge (78 and 79). Note that the bridge has been rebuilt between the taking of the photographs, with a new deck on the original piers. Both the crossings were on typical GNSR bridges which still survive. Later, the Fiddich is crossed just south and east of Dufftown by a masonry viaduct of two arches of 60 feet. This is at the point where the line abruptly changes general direction from south west to north west.

78   Newton Bridge between Craigellachie and Dufftown (AS)

Dufftown 3m 67c (322415, OS sheet 26, Elgin)

By road from Craigellachie take the A941 towards Keith, and Dufftown station is on the left just north of the Glenfiddich distillery and immediately south of the Convalmore distillery.

On the Speyside Way we follow the trackbed away from the road bridges and Fiddich Park (the site of Craigellachie station), passing the sites of the signal box on the left and the turntable on the right. This is the Dufftown spur of the Speyside Way and is easy walking even though it is uphill to just beyond Newton Bridge, about the halfway point. Excellent views of the Fiddich in its gorge, which has been likened to the Pass of Killiccrankie, can be obtained during this walk. The gorge is heavily wooded with mixed coniferous and deciduous trees, and there are many shrubs and bushes. The nature of the terrain meant that the line descended from Newton Bridge by means of short sharp curves and numerous cuttings and embankments. Abundant plants and flowers may be found along this part of the walk. In the more open parts will be found wild roses, rowan, rosebay willow herb and common mullein; and in the deep cuttings, ferns of many types, wood avens, wild strawberries and, for the sharp-eyed observer, spotted orchids.

Just past the sites of the old signal box (on the left overlooking the river, 26 and Map 2) and the turntable pit (on the right) the Speyside Way crosses the Fiddich for the first time on a fine GNSR girder bridge. It has steel girders laid on a central stone pillar and two abutments. Shortly after this the line passes under a road bridge which, at the time of writing, is being repaired. The Speyside Way temporarily climbs the embankment (note the base of a GNSR signal close to the footpath) and crosses the road. Upon regaining the railway track our path passes, on the right, a disused distillery which is in ruins (80), and much overgrown, and then plunges into a rocky gorge.

The path rises all the way, mostly in cutting but occasionally on embankments, to Newton Bridge about two miles from Craigellachie where the Fiddich is crossed by a magnificent skew bridge (78 and 79). Good views of this bridge are obtainable from the banks at both ends. It has two stone abutments and two central piers and is similar to many GNSR bridges except that it is considerably higher. From a short way past Newton Bridge the going is downhill all the way to Dufftown. The Speyside Way ends by the Convalmore distillery immediately north of Dufftown Station. Rejoin the A941 for the remainder of the journey.

The station building at Dufftown (Map 10, 81 and 82) is extant

79 Newton Bridge looking towards Craigellachie, August 1986 (RRFK)

80 Trackbed south of Craigellachie looking towards Dufftown, August 1986 (RRFK)

81 Dufftown looking towards Craigellachie (LOS)

82 Dufftown, August 1986 (LOS)

83 Dufftown station building, August 1986 (RRFK)

84 Drummuir looking towards Keith (LOS)

85   Drummuir, August 1986 (RRFK)

and used as a headquarters for the Community Projects Service. The name 'Dufftown' is in gold letters on the glass panel over the door to the platform (83). Although there is only one track both platforms still exist. However, the Elgin-bound platform, which is stone built, has been cut short just past the station building. The other platform is wooden, rotting rapidly and covered with vegetation. The building which it once supported is no more, although its base is to be found. The station master's house, slightly to the north of the station, is still occupied and there are three goods sidings for grain traffic still in use to the immediate south of the station.

The only passenger traffic is the summer only, twice weekly *Northern Belle*. This is an excursion from Aberdeen with lunch and tea served on the train and visits to either the Glenfiddich distillery or Drummuir House (not normally open to the public). Dufftown is famous for its distilleries (the local saying is 'Rome was built on seven hills but Dufftown was built on seven stills'). Many of these distilleries welcome visitors. The tour around the Glenfiddich Distillery includes and excellent audio-visual presentation, an informative, well conducted tour of all parts of the distillery and a wee dram.

Dufftown was founded in 1817 by the 4th Earl of Fife, James Duff. Between the town and the station is the thirteen-century Balvenie Castle which is reached by taking the B road between the A941 and the B9014 about half a mile south of the station. It is a courtyard castle, probably begun in the thirteenth century. It has associations with Edward I of England; Mary Queen of Scots; the Earls of Atholl; the Marquis of Montrose, and the Jacobites, who occupied it in 1689 after the Battle of Killiecrankie. It is said, possibly incorrectly, that the castle is of Danish origin. It is open from April to September, Thursdays to Sundays.

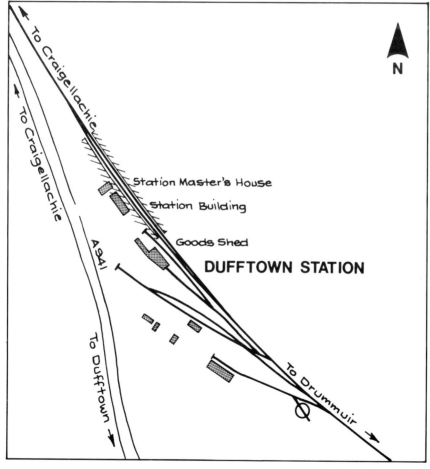

Map 10 Dufftown

In the centre of the town is a crossroads in the midst of which is the castellated Clocktower, erected in 1839, having previously been in Banff. It was known as the 'hanging clock', or 'the clock that hanged MacPherson', because an Earl of Fife, Lord Braco, had advanced the clock so that the execution of a local malefactor, MacPherson of Kingussie (a freebooter who was popular with the people but not with his lordship), occurred before the reprieve reached Banff. The clock was later transferred to the Dufftown tower which has been variously, town jail, Burgh Chambers, and is now the tourist information centre and museum. The first president of the Canadian Pacific Railroad, George Stephen, Lord Mountstephen, was born in Dufftown.

In the town is Mortlach Parish Church, one of the oldest places of Christian worship in Scotland. It was allegedly founded in 566 by St Moluag. Although substantially reconstructed in 1876 and 1931, portions of the old building have survived, both in the church and graveyard. From here it is only a short walk to Maisters Wood and Well.

One and a half miles south east of Dufftown is Auchindoun Castle, a three-storey-high keep surrounded by Pictish earthworks, dating from the fifteenth century.

To the south west of Dufftown are the shattered granite twin summits of Ben Rinnes. Access is from the B9009 to Tomintoul, and on a clear day extensive views may be obtained.

Besides a variety of shops, eating places and accommodation, there are facilities for fishing, golf, bowls, tennis, walking, camping and picnicking.

Mortlach Branch

Before proceeding further along the mainline towards Keith we can take a small diversion to investigate the remains of the Mortlach branch. This branch was built, probably without Parliamentary approval, to serve some ditilleries near to Dufftown.

Although the main line to Dufftown still exists this branch line to the distilleries south of the town has been dismantled. It used to leave the main line just east of where the main line crosses the B9014 at the conclusion of the big curve in that line and at the end of the brick viaduct (17). The branch was opened in stages between 1891 and 1900 and closed between 1964 and 1966. It was solely for goods.

Parkmore 14c from junction (330408, OS sheet 28, Elgin)

This opened on 5 October 1891 as Parkbeg Lime Sidings, but after that was referred to as Parkmore Lime Works Siding. It closed on 7 November 1966.

Glendullan 31c (331402, OS sheet 28, Elgin)

This was opened in 1900 and closed on 7 November 1966.

Crachie 60c (331398, OS sheet 28, Elgin)

The remains of a level crossing can be seen at this point.

Mortlach 1m 3c (327397, OS sheet 28, Elgin)

This opened in 1900 but closed on 23 March 1964.

One can now rejoin our exploration of the main line from Dufftown to Keith.

From Dufftown to Keith the railway is still in use (1986) and cannot be walked. However one can visit all the stations by road. (N.B.: Some authorities give the closure of this section as 6 June 1983, but it was in use by the *Northern Belle* for two or three summers following that.)

Leave Dufftown on the B9014 and head towards Keith.

The railway line is on the left of the B9014 and passes close to Loch Park, three miles north of Dufftown. At this point the line is in a deep wooded cutting, partially visible from the road. Loch Park, a well known local beauty spot, is an artificial lake in the grounds of Drummuir House and was formed by damming the river Isla, whose source it now is. At this point the wide Strathisla has narrowed down and the railway clings to a ledge along Loch Park. The *Northern Belle* normally halts here to allow passengers to enjoy the very pretty woodland lake.

Drummuir Curlers Platform (362435, OS sheet 28, Elgin)

The curler's platform is referred to in company minutes of 12 December 1894: 'A platform to be provided at the north end of the loch.' No evidence of its existence is perceivable today.

Past the end of Loch Park an occupation bridge over the line can be seen with Drummuir Castle in the trees beyond.

Drummuir 8m 16c (378443, OS sheet 28, Elgin)

Continue along the B9014 past Drummuir Estate sawmill on the right and 100 yards further on turn left taking the unclassified road at 376439 and turning left at the Y-junction about a quarter of a mile further on. The site of the station entrance is between the road crossing of the river and the railway.

The line became double by the bridge to serve two platforms (84). One of these is still discernible but all the buildings have been demolished. The other platform is heavily overgrown (85). The remains of a goods platform can be seen.

Leave the station and turn left at the junction. As one rejoins the B9014 there is a road sign to Drummuir Station (86). Turn left and continue north east on the B9014. After here Strathisla widens out and the passage for the railway becomes easier.

Towiemore 9m 49c (395456, OS sheet 28, Elgin)

About half a mile after the road goes under a substantial stone bridge, pass a large stone on the left and turn right beside the houses just before an S-bend opposite Lower Towie Farm (393457). The station is a quarter of a mile further on where this track crosses the line and a small tributary of the Isla.

This station opened before 1 June 1863 as Drummuir Lime Kilns Siding. By December 1884 it had been renamed Botriphine. It was closed on 10 July 1890 and then reopened in 1894. It was renamed once again on 1 January 1898. This time it was called Towiemore. A passenger service was available from about 1924 but it was not in the public timetable until 1937. A working circular of 18 April 1924 mentions laying down a van body.

The most unusual and delightful station buildings (87 and 88) were still extant in 1985 consisting of a concrete hut with two doors, similar to that at Knockando, and a small dismounted coach, probably off an old four wheeler. This originally comprised four compartments. One of these was the bookinghall with a ticket window and door cut in the partition, and the other compartments had been made into an office for the 'station master'. Electric lighting and a stove had been fitted at one time. The outside of the coach still bore the traces of paint, red on the lower panels and cream on the upper. Unfortunately BR sold the coach body to a farmer in Huntly to use as a shed, and this unique 'building' has been removed leaving a rather forlorn little station (89).

The platform has been almost totally erased and has become simply a bank, covered in nettles and rose bay willow herb, leading up from the track. Behind the station are the remains of the very extensive goods sidings.

Return to the B9014 and turn right.

Auchindachy 11m 11c (406476, OS sheet 28, Elgin)

Shortly after the S-bend where the road passes over the railway, and immediately before the river bridge, the entrance to Auchindachy station is on the left. It is marked by a pair of GNSR gates and gateposts which are in good condition. The drive, station house and station building are private, but there is room to park by the roadside just on the other side of the river bridge.

From its opening this station (Map 11) was known as Botriphine, as was Towiemore twenty-one years after this station ceased to be Botriphine and became Auchindachy, which had occurred by 1 June 1863. The stone station building, at the far end of the private drive, is derelict but standing. The doors are open and one can walk through on to theplatform. The building is in very poor condition with the roof leaking and timbers rotting. It consists of three main rooms, the outer of which had lathe and plaster walls with plaster ceilings and cornice. (see sketch plan). The central room had vertical planking halfway up the walls with the brick work painted on the rear and right hand side walls. The other walls are vertical planking all the way to the ceiling. The roof has visible rafters, crossbeams and kingpins, all painted (see typical lineside features in section I).

Continue on the B9014 into Keith.

Keith Town 13m 78c (429508, OS sheet 28, Elgin)

Turn right onto the A95. Immediately after the road crosses the railway turn sharp left and the station entrance is down a gravel track on the left at this point.

The steps from this track and the car park are heavily overgrown as is the whole of the station. All the buildings have been destroyed and all that remains is the platform, a signal and the station name board (91 and 92). Although the letters have been removed the name is still legible. From the platform the view to the left is restricted by the road overbridge, whilst that to the right shows the track passing the signal, crossing a stream on a standard GNSR girder bridge, and curving to the left to be lost in the trees. A better view of the bridge can be obtained by climbing down by the river, but the undergrowth is extremely deep. In the distance between the trees can be seen the distinctive roof of a distillery. This station was called Earlsmill until 1 May 1897 and was always purely a passenger station and is more convenient for the town than the Junction station which is the only one is use for the people of Keith.

Turn left onto the A95.

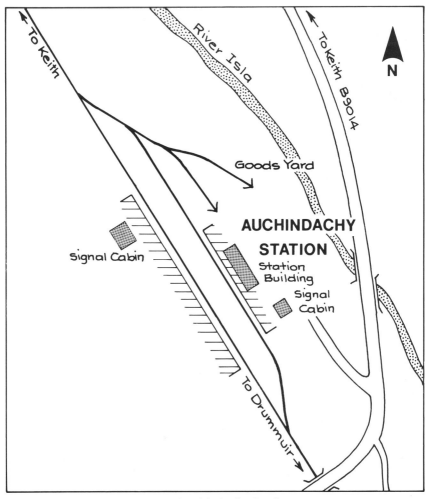

Map 11 Auchindachy Station

86   Road sign to Drummuir station, August 1986 (RRFK)

87   Towiemore looking towards Keith, June 1957 (JLS)

88   Towiemore, July 1985 (RRFK)

89   Towiemore, August 1986 (RRFK)

90   Auchindachy looking towards Keith, August 1986 (RRFK)

Keith Junction 14m 42c (430516, OS sheet 28, Elgin)

Turn left onto the B9116 from the A95 and follow the signs to the station.

This station was the furthest west the GNSR went on the direct Aberdeen to Inverness route. The station still sees regular traffic with trains between those cities calling there. In addition there is an extensive goods yard and a considerable amount of freight traffic is handled. The ex-GNSR line to Dufftown has its own single platform on the south of the station (93 and 94). The branch curves away and rises steeply from the mainline. Keith station was in the shape of a Vee with the GNSR and HR platforms forming the two sides of the Vee. The Highland has a windshield on the far side of the track, partially supported by girders from the canopy. The buildings were at the broad end, while at the pointed end were two terminal platforms with steel and glass canopies (95 and 96). The station has been simplified with the terminal tracks between the HR and GNSR platforms having been removed.

The town of Keith dates from at least AD 700 and it was nearby that the Jacobites fought their last successful action, defeating a

91   Keith Town looking towards Keith (LOS)

92   Keith Town, August 1986 (RRFK)

93 Keith Junction GNSR platform. Courtesy Real Photograph Co.

94 Keith Junction Speyside platform looking towards Aberdeen, August 1986 (RRFK)

95 Keith Junction looking towards Elgin. Courtesy Real Photograph Co.

96   Keith Junction, August 1986 (RRFK)

section of the army of the Duke of Cumberland (Stinking Billy or Sweet William depending upon your loyalties). The main industries are the manufacture of woollen goods and the distilling of whisky. G & G Kynoch's Isla Park Mills and the Strathisla distillery are open to the public and have guided tours, visitors' centres and shops. The two oldest places of interest are the Milton Tower (built in 1480) which is in Station Road and the pack-horse bridge, just off Regent Street. This bridge, built in 1609, is the oldest in Morayshire and one of the oldest in Scotland. The churches of Holy Trinity, St Rufus and St Thomas are all well worth a visit. About 5½ miles outside the town is Eggs & Co, where egg decoration can be seen.

Facilities are available for golf, fishing, swimming, bowls and tennis. Many good walks can be undertaken from Keith. It has a comprehensive selection of shops, eating places, accommodation, etc.

V

Craigellachie to Elgin and Lossiemouth

History of the section

This line (Map 12) is 12 miles 46 chains long from Craigellachie to Elgin and a further 5 miles 63 chains to Lossiemouth. The original powers were obtained on 16 July 1846 for a line from Lossiemouth to Elgin and then from Orton (on the proposed GNSR) to Craigellachie. The delay in constructing the GNSR meant that the powers for the Orton to Craigellachie section were abandoned on 10 July 1851. The remaining section joining Elgin with the coast was opened on 10 August 1852. The Inverness and Aberdeen Junction Railway (I&AJR) had by this time built a line to Keith, and the Morayshire railway obtained an Act to construct the line from Orton to Craigellachie (14 July 1852). This line opened to Rothes on 23 August 1858 and to Craigellachie on 23 December 1858. The actual terminus of this line was at Dandaleith although until 1865 it was called Craigellachie.

Morayshire Railway trains, pulled by their own locomotives, ran over the I&AJR tracks between Elgin and Orton. This arrangement lasted only six weeks because of I&AJR complaints about MR engines and MR trains were taken between the two halves of the Morayshire Railway by I&AJR locomotives. This was unsatisfactory for the Morayshire line and on 3 July 1860 the Glen of Rothes Railway obtained its Act to build an independent line between Elgin and Rothes. This opened for goods on 30 December 1861 and for passengers on 1 January 1862. The points at Orton were removed by the Moray line immediately their independent route from Elgin to Rothes was opened. This was to deny the Highland line access to the Spey valley. However, the tracks were left *in situ* and not removed until 1907 (map 14).

On 17 May 1861 the Morayshire line was authorised to cross the Spey and join up with the Strathspey Railway which obtained its Act

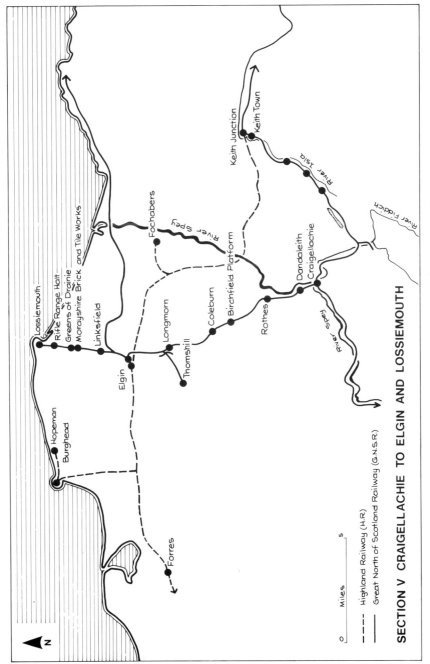

Map 12 Craigellachie to Elgin and Lossiemouth

Lossiemouth
Rifle Range Halt
Greens of Drainie
Morayshire Brick and Tile Works
Linksfield
Fochabers
River Spey
Keith Junction
Keith Town
River Isla
River Fiddich
Dandaleith
Craigellachie
Longmorn
Coleburn
Birchfield Platform
Rothes
Thomshill
Elgin
River Spey
Hopeman
Burghead
Forres

N

Miles
0   5

- - - - - Highland Railway (H.R.)
———————— Great North of Scotland Railway (G.N.S.R.)

SECTION V CRAIGELLACHIE TO ELGIN AND LOSSIEMOUTH

on the same date. The line from Craigellachie (Dandaleith after 1865) to Strathspey Junction (Craigellachie after 1865) was opened on 1 July 1863. Powers for the Morayshire line to amalgamate with the GNSR were obtained on 30 July 1866. These were ratified by an Act of 1 August 1881 and the union took place as from 1 October 1881.

When this line opened the only distillery was one at Rothes but by 1884 the Glenrothes and Glenlossie distilleries were open and the Glenspey distillery at Rothes opened in 1885. Between 1890 and 1898 six more distilleries opened along the section of line between Elgin and Craigellachie.

At Longmorn three distilleries were served by branches from that station. The longest branch was to the Glenlossie distillery, one and a half miles away at Thomshill, which seems to have been built without parliamentary approval.

The Glenlossie branch closed many years before the main line: however, when the main line was closed the other two branches were still in use. The Benriach & Longmorn Railway continued in use as an isolated railway using a four-wheeled diesel mechanical locomotive, four vans and two open wagons for distillery use. The track work was all GNSR with two sorts of chair, a small type dated 1876 and a normal one dated 1890, and rails marked 'Barrow, GNSR 1876'.

This little railway closed on Friday 29 February 1980 and the Strathspey railway have removed the track. The vans and engine may have followed the rail on which they ran for so many years while the wagons may have found a new home and useful life with the Brechin Railway Preservation Society.

Services on the Craigellachie to Elgin section were closely related to those on the Keith to Craigellachie but with the occasional goods train omitted. The mainline closed for passengers on 6 May 1968 and for goods on Friday, 1 November the same year.

Lossiemouth branch services in 1902 were eleven trains per day each way of which one was mixed and two were solely for goods traffic. However, by 1931 the service was nearly halved to two mixed, four passenger and no goods trains. The 1951 timetable shows two mixed and two passenger services from Elgin. The branch closed on 6 April 1964.

This section is not part of the Speyside Way and is private property. Access by road only is described. Comments on the possible suitability of the line for walking are given, but permission of the various landowners will be required before it is attempted. The countryside in this section north of Craigellachie is quite different to that of the Spey Valley or of the wooded gorge of the Fiddich. Here one finds much more open, arable land, with planted coniferous coppices. The landscape opens out towards the coast.

Dandaleith 0m 50c (287460, OS sheet 28, Elgin)

Just past the turning for Archiestown (B9102) turn right for Dandaleith Farm. The new course of the A941 has obliterated the station (Map 13; 97) but the old retaining wall is clearly visible from the farm (98), surrounded by young conifers. The old road has become a layby (105).

The trackbed from the abutments of the Spey Viaduct, and Craigellachie, to Dandaleith station is clearly visible but very overgrown, especially near the river. From here to Rothes the old line looks as if it can be walked nearly all the way, with the exception of the odd section which has been ploughed out.

Take the A941 from Craigellachie towards Rothes.

Rothes 2m 68c (279494, OS sheet 28, Elgin)

Follow the A941 towards Elgin. In the centre of Rothes turn right at the Station Hotel. The station has been completely levelled and a lorry park constructed on its site (Maps 14 and 14a; 99 and 100). However, the distillery seen on the photographs is still there. Note how the station developed as shown in Maps 14 and 14a.

Walkers can follow the line from the southern outskirts of Rothes to the site of the old station. The last recognisable feature of the railway is the small bridge over the Burn of Rothes, which is now a footbridge.

Beyond the lorry park the trackbed may be regained by turning off on to a sidetrack at the junction of the A941 and B9105. A little way down this track are two bridges over a stream. These may mark the sites of the lines to Elgin and Orton (Map 14). The railway bridge over the A941 has been removed.

Rothes is a small town situated on the Spey between Ben Aigan and Conerock Hill. It has anumber of shops, restaurants and hotels. There are facilities for tennis, bowls, pony trekking and riding. Founded in 1766 as a crofting township, industry came in the mid nineteenth century with the building of the Glen Grant distillery. This is open May to October, Monday to Friday. At one time there were five distilleries in the town. A massive wall is all that remains of Rothes Castle, stronghold of the Leslie family until 1622, the stones reputedly having been used to build houses in the village. The Leslies later sold the castle to the Earl of Seafield.

Continue along the A941 to Elgin.

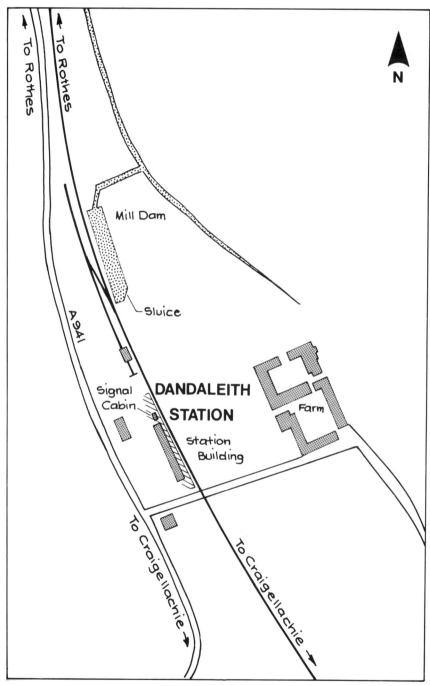

Map 13 Dandaleith

97 Dandaleith, Craigellachie to the left. L&GRP courtesy David & Charles

98 Dandaleith, August 1986 (RRFK)

99 Rothes looking towards Elgin. Courtesy Real Photograph Co.

100   Rothes looking towards Craigellachie (LOS)

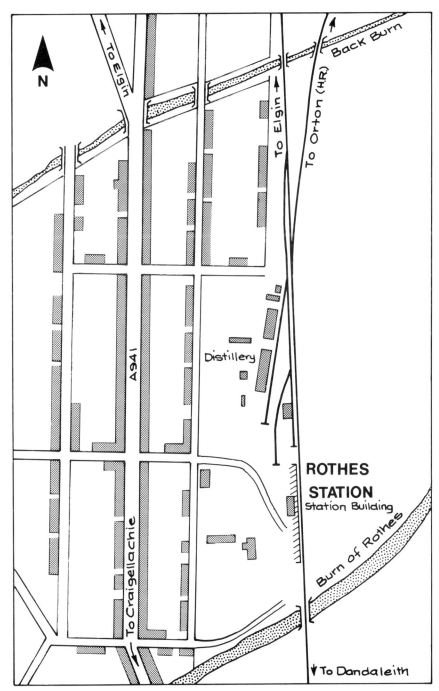

Map 14 Rothes in GNSR days

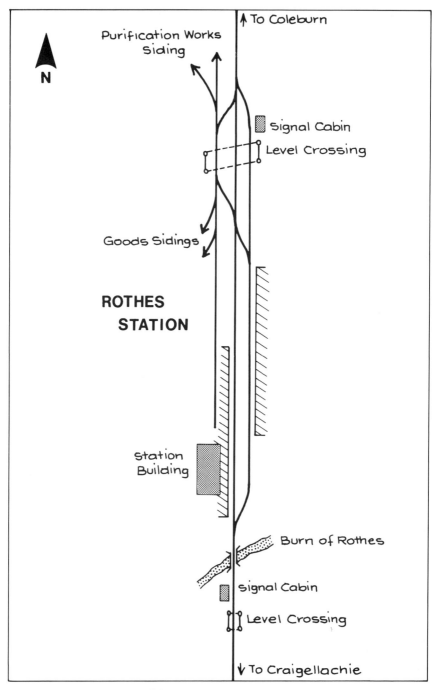

To Coleburn

Purification Works
Siding

N

Signal Cabin
Level Crossing

Goods Sidings

**ROTHES
STATION**

Station
Building

Burn of Rothes

Signal Cabin

Level Crossing

To Craigellachie

Map 14a Rothes in 1933

Birchfield Platform 5m 75c (255533, OS sheet 28, Elgin)

For walkers the trackbed from Rothes should be clear to walk. Drivers take a very small turning on the right after the second entrance (most northerly) to the Rothes Glen Hotel (on the left). The turning is opposite the hotel sign and has a small notice almost hidden by trees, saying 'Birchfield Crossing'.

After a short drive through a young plantation one comes to the old railway which has some sleepers and fencing *in situ* (Map 15). There is no evidence of the station (102) but by the line and track from the road is a recently rebuilt house which may be the old station

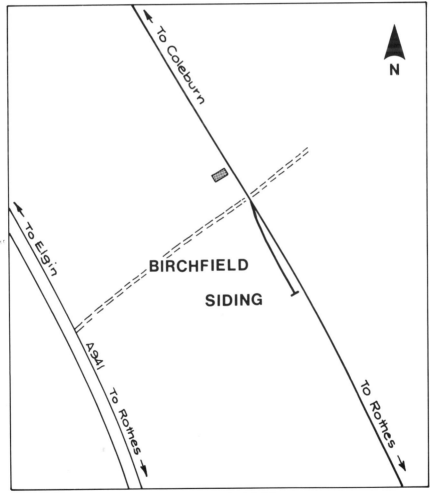

Map 15 Birchfield

101 Birchfield Platform looking towards Craigellachie, October 1952 (JLS)

102 Birchfield Platform looking towards Elgin, August 1986 (RRFK)

house (102, taken from the opposite direction to 101). The main part of the lower storey has thick walls and has the same ground plan as other railway cottages. The new additions have much thinner walls. It is certainly the house in photo 101.

The trackbed can be clearly discerned in both directions as well as the possible site of the siding. The trackbed is grassy and easy to walk.

The earliest reference was in the timetable of December 1884. First edition OS maps show a goods siding (Map 16) but by 1904 it was passenger only.

Return to the A941 and turn right to Elgin.

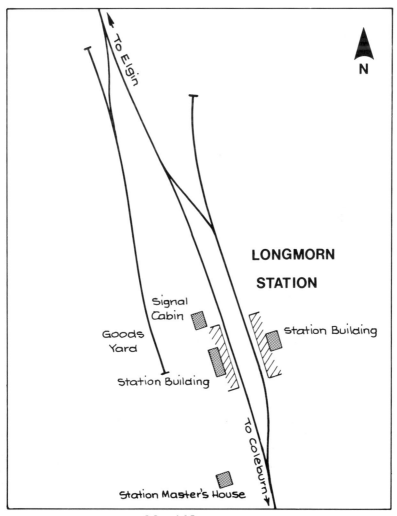

Map 16 Longmorn

Coleburn Goods 7m 19c (241553, OS sheet 28, Elgin)

Car drivers should turn off the A941, immediately after a row of cottages into Coleburn distillery. Drive through the wooded grounds turning left and right between the buildings. This is a through road to a farm on the east of the railway.

For walkers attempting to come from the south along the line there is a wooden footbridge replacing the demolished railway bridge. A hundred yards after that bridge is the base of a signal box where the line widened for the junction of the distillery branch which passed through the gates on the left of the main line (103 and 104). The main line passed east of the distillery in a shallow cutting. At the end of this the line crosses the small road to the farm. By this crossing are kissing gates and a railway house, now the Customs and Excise office.

The goods siding rises quite steeply up to the distillery and widens to two tracks at a loading bay immediately behind the buildings and above the Customs and Excise building, the roof of which is just visible (105). On the loading bay is the base of a crane and to the left is a steep drop to the weighbridge and storehouse. Coal and grain came in and whisky went out via these sidings. The fullbarrels were weighed outside the store and hoisted up into the waiting wagons. The shadow of an oil tank, built over one of the sidings is visible.

This is a good example of the close relationship which existed between the railway and the distilleries in this area. The siding has been incorporated in the design of the building.

The trackbed runs north from the crossing for about 200 yards before being ploughed up for a quarter of a mile. Most of the trackbed in this area is hedged and fenced and surrounded by farmland. Here again vegetation is lush. Then the track runs into a deep wooded cutting. The trackbed is by a stream and a stone retaining wall can be seen from the A941. Some of the line has been ploughed up near Fogwatt.

Longmorn 9m 42c (235585, OS sheet 28, Elgin)

Turn east off the A941 to the village of Longmorn at 230582. On the left of this side road can be seen the remains, including a bridge over a small stream, of one of the three goods branches running from north of Longmorn station to distilleries nearby. Drive past the distillery and immediately before the dismantled bridge turn sharp left. The station is 100 yards ahead. It is the private property of Longmorn distillery. For walkers, although the railway bridge over the stream has been demolished there is a bridge of sleepers.

One theory is that the name Longmorn is derived from the Welsh 'lhanmorgund' or 'Morgan the Holy man'. The water for the distillery comes from a local spring which never dries up, while the peat comes from the nearby Mannoch Hill.

Here is a pleasant discovery for this station is the most intact of any on these three lines (Map 16; 106 and 107). It has both platforms, with coal stored on the trackbed between them, the main station building (108) on the north (Elgin) bound platform and a waiting shelter on the other. All the buildings are glazed, painted cream and brown and padlocked. The waiting shelter is made of vertical wooden boards whilst the main building is also wooden on a stone base. This is over 6 feet high at the rear as the ground drops steeply away (1). It has a central room with central double doors and one smaller room on each sife. The gentlemen's toilet is at the north end.There was no outside access to the rear of the building. This set of buildings gives an excellent impression of how many GNSR stations must have looked.

Behind the main building, to the northwest of the station, is a goods loading platform with a GNSR lamp holder. North of the station is a level crossing gate, closed across the trackbed with its red disc still clearly visible. To the southwest of the station is the station master's house which is occupied.

The junction of the three sidings to other distilleries was north of Longmorn station. The longest was that seen by the side road on the way in. It ran 1 mile 40 chains to the Glenlossie distillery at Thomshill. The others were to Benriach distillery (25 chains) and to Longmorn distillery itself.

Walkers might be able to attempt to follow the line to Elgin. Car drivers return to A941 and turn right towards Elgin. Immediately after this junction the main road crosses the old goods branch to the distillery at Thomshill (see historical introduction at the start of this section).

The countryside here is more open, arable land with scattered settlements and farms. Clumps of coniferous trees have been planted, especially around the distilleries. From the road glimpses of the trackbed can be seen on the right, down in the valley.

Elgin 12m 46c (221622, OS sheet 28, Elgin)

Drive north on the A941 until the last turning in Elgin before the large bridge over the Highland line in the centre of the city. Turn right and then first left over a bridge crossing the HR. Looking left,

103   Coleburn Goods looking towards Elgin, October 1954 (JLS)

104   Coleburn Goods looking towards Elgin, August 1986 (RRFK)

105   Coleburn Goods, top of loading bay, August 1986 (RRFK)

106   Longmorn looking towards Elgin, October 1954 (JLS)

107   Longmorn looking towards Elgin, August 1986 (RRFK)

108   Longmorn station building, August 1986 (RRFK)

good views of the GNSR station can be obtained and the junction of the two railways seen. Continue and take the first right into Ashgrove Road. At the end turn right into a housing estate and stop when the road turns left. Walk ahead over the pedestrain bridge over the HR. All that is left of the GNSR bridge over the HR can be seen on the left. There are the stone abutments with a pipe between them. For any walkers who have managed to get from Longmorn this would be a good point to regain the road.

Return to Ashgrove Road and bear right. The GNSR viaduct has been demolished and partly built upon to provide a Grampian Regional Council depot. A buffer stop can be seen at the end of the embankment which leads to the now gone bridge.

Continue until the A96 is reached. At this point on the immediate left the coast line and that to Lossiemouth crossed the A96 but it is now totally obliterated by new industrial buildings. Turn left and left again at the roundabout to reach Elgin Station.

The station building (109 and 110) is in very good condition and largely unaltered, being used as a freight headquarters. (Cf Highland Station a quarter of a mile down the road to the west which, although still used by passengers, has had its buildings demolished and 'bus-type shelters' erected. Do obtain permission before wandering around the station. Walk to the east end of the station and round the back where one can gain access to the platform, from whence it is possible to walk through to the Highland station. The through GNSR platform, the circulating area and the glass canopies (111 and 112) over these are still extant but the terminal platforms at the east of the station have been removed.

The large signal box opposite the through platform is still in use. The beautiful booking hall with its original woodwork and stained glass is in excellent condition (113 and 114). Note particularly the polished wood barriers by the former ticket windows, and, looking up, the elaborate plaster pendants hanging from the glazed vaulting. The wooden goods shed (115 and 116) at the east end and north of the old terminal platforms is still in use and, although battered, retains its cream and brown livery. The yard seemed to be packed with plastic bags marked 'store in the dry'. This during the wettest summer this century in Scotland! Note the impressive signals and the GNSR goods break van (or road van) on the left (115).

The medieval town plan of Elgin is still discernibleIn the market place is a Muckle Cross erected in 1650, and restored in 1888. Its cathedral, the 'Lantern of the North', has had a chequered history. It was built in 1224, burnt down in 1390, restored and then allowed to decay since 1771, the Protestants having no use for such a building.

When complete it was nearly 300 feet long and had towers at the west end 84 feet high. The remains are now in the care of the Government who are stopping any further deterioration and have provided a helpful information centre. The octagonal chapter house has been restored and re-roofed. Adjacent is the Bishop's House (in better repair than the Cathedral in spite of the Presbyterians disliking Bishops even more than their seats). The Cathedral and the Bishop's House are approached through well-tended Cooper Park, which also contains the elegant library with a collection of Morayshire photographs, including some of the GNSR.

Also worth seeing in Elgin or nearby are The Elgin Museum, Braco's Banking House, Masonic Close, Old Mills watermill and visitors centre, Dr Gray's Hospital, Spynie Palace (formerly the seat of the Bishops in Moray but uninhabited since the end of the seventeenth century and now a ruin) and churchyard, Duffus Castle at Old Duffus and Pluscarden Abbey. This was founded in 1230 but fell into disuse after the reformation. The Benedictine community was able to take up residence again after nearly 400 years in 1948. Not far to the west is the original Dallas.

Thus the City of Elgin, with many shops, restaurants, hotels and facilities for golf, swimming, fishing, bowls and tennis makes an excellent centre—poised between the coast and the countryside.

Walkers may wish to attempt to follow the line to Lossiemouth, all the relevant permissions having been obtained. The line immediately north of Elgin station has been completely obliterated; however, it can be joined farther north.

From the station walk back to the roundabout, cross the A96 and follow the signs to the Cathedral. Following the road to the right, take the right turn to Pitgaveny and Calcots. Half a mile on is the site of a demolished bridge by the junction of the coast and Lossiemouth lines. Much of the coast line has been ploughed up but there is a distant view of an isolated bridge. Follow the straight track to the north through flat countryside.

Linksfield 14m 22c (231647, OS sheet 28. Elgin)

The site of a level crossing with a small building next to the track. There was a halt here by 1858 but it closed on 1 December 1859.

Morayshire Brick and Tile Works Siding 16m 2c (234673, OS sheet 28, Elgin)

The site of a private siding to this works.

109 Elgin GNSR station exterior. Courtesy Real Photograph Co.

110 Elgin GNSR station, August 1986 (RRFK)

111 Elgin GNSR station main line platform in LNER days.
Courtesy Real Photograph Co.

112   Elgin GNSR station platform, August 1986 (RRFK)

113 Elgin GNSR station interior, August 1986 (RRFK)

114 Elgin GNSR station interior, August 1986 (RRFK)

115 Elgin GNSR station looking towards Inverness.
Courtesy Real Photograph Co.

116   Elgin GNSR station, August 1986 (RRFK)

Greens of Drainie 16m 19c (234677, OS sheet 28, Elgin)

A small halt at a level crossing which was open by 1858 but was closed on 1 December 1859.

Rifle Range Halt 17m 36c (236697, OS sheet 28, Elgin)

This was provided in 1913 for the Territorial Army and was dismantled in 1932. There is no road access to the site of this halt.

Lossiemouth (see later)

Car drivers are recommended to make a detour to visit nearby Fochabers. Leave Elgin Station and return to the roundabout, turn right on to the A96 towards Fochabers.

Fochabers (HR) (338597, OS sheet 28, Elgin)

Just past the famous Baxters factory turn right by an electricity substation, just before crossing the Spey. Turn left into a small estate (Luchberry Road) and left again. Follow the road to the left and the station (117 and 118) is straight ahead. One is approaching it from the track side. It is now called Douglas Lodge and looks as if it could be a hostel. There is an excellent view of the station in the aerial photograph in the visitors centre at Baxters factory.

At Fochabers are the ruins of Gordon Castle; also Baxters (fruit and preserves merchants) visitors centre, open weekdays April to October, and the Folk Museum, open 9.30am to 5.30pm. There are also bowls, golf, tennis, swimming and fishing.

Return on the A96 towards Elgin.

Lossiemouth 18m 24c (238708, OS sheet 28, Elgin)

In Elgin take the A941 to Lossiemouth. Access to the intermediate places may be available as follows: for Linksfield crossing turn right at map reference 217645 and left at 219642; for Morayshire Brickworks, turn right at 228672; for Greens of Drainie turn right at 229678. Spynie Palace and Spynie Churchyard are between the road and the old track. The massive ruins of the palace of the Bishops of

117   Fochabers Town station (HR) (LOS)

118   Fochabers station, August 1986 (RRFK)

Moray are not open to the public, but can be seen from the Spynie Canal bridge on this road. James Ramsay MacDonald, first Labour Prime Minister of Britain is buried in Spynie Churchyard.

Follow the road towards the busy fishing harbour. The station is just beyond the sandspit and the entrance of the river Lossie and the Spynie Canal into the sea where there are very attractive promenade gardens.

Once there was a large station building (Map 17; 119) but all that remains is a curved passengerplatform inside a wall, which is next to the road, and an island platform which served two goods lines (120 and 122). Note the array of chimney pots at the Elgin end of the station building (119 and 120).

An unusual feature of the train operations at Lossiemouth station was the ringing of a handbell to announce the departure of a train. Upon the closure of the line the bell was given to a local fishmarket.

The base of a signal and crane are visible. The station buildings are no more. The platforms end at the harbour but the rails went on another 5 chains to the quayside.

There is the Lossiemouth Fisheries and Community Museum, sandy beaches, golf, fishing, tennis, bowls and swimming. Lossiemouth is a busy little town with useful shops and eating places.

Continue north on the A941 and turn left onto the B9040. At 159617 turn left onto the B9012 and drive to Duffus. Here are a fifteenth century castle and a thirteenth century church. Nearby is Gordonstoun School. Return to the B9040 and head for Burghead, for another excursion into HR territory.

Hopeman (HR) (145697, OS sheet 28, Elgin)

Turn off the B9040 at 146694 to Newtown; the HR station was west or left of the road, a short way before the harbour. The station site is now a caravan park with station buildings intact (122 and 123), largely unchanged outwardly, being used as the administrative centre, loos, etc. There are sandy beaches, bowls, sea angling, golf and seabathing.

Return to the B9040.

Burghead (HR) (115688, OS sheet 28, Elgin)

Turn right onto the B9012 and then right onto the B9089, the road crosses the railway immediatelyeast of the station. The entrance to the railway yard is on the left just over the bridge. The railway from

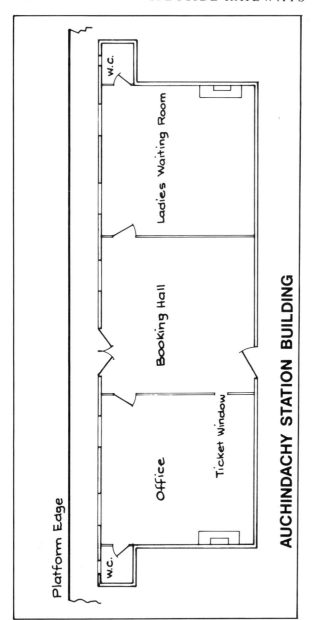

AUCHINDACHY STATION BUILDING

Map 17 Auchindachy Station Building.
1. Exterior. Remains of clock mounting on outside wall facing platform. Centre section of wall facing platform, wooden construction.
2. Interior. *Office* Round topped fireplace. Roof rafters, cross-beams and king-pins visible. Painted vertical planking half way up—then painted brick on two walls. Platform wall and partition wall to Booking Hall are constructed of vertical planks. *Booking Hall* Ceiling with plaster cornices still intact. Some exposed lathe and plaster walls. *Ladies Waiting Room* Lathe and plaster walls and ceiling with cornices as Booking Hall. Square topped fireplace.

the main line is still in use as a single track goods branch to just east of Burghead station but has been lifted from there to Hopeman. The station building (124, 125 and 126) is still extant, painted light blue and used as a transport depot. Unfortunately the view of it has been obscured by a new building. Be very careful if approaching the track at this point as some goods trains still pass.

Burghead was the birthplace of Ramsay MacDonald, Britain's first socialist Prime Minister, and has a Museum of Archaeology.

Leave on the B9089 and head south through the Roseisle Forest. At the cross roads at 124657 continue on the unclassified road to Crook of Alves on the A96(T). From here there is a choice of places to visit. To the west is Forres, famous for the work of its gardens department, and Brodie Castle (NT) a couple of miles further west, or to the south of Monaughty Forest, on the unclassified roads, is Pluscarden Abbey dating from 1230. Further west is Cawdor Castle, home of the Thanes of Cawdor since the fourteenth century. This is open from May to September.

Lossiemouth Station. A holiday Scene.

119 Lossiemouth station (MDL)

120 Lossiemouth station looking from Elgin. Courtesy Real Photograph Co.

121   Lossiemouth station, August 1986 (RRFK)

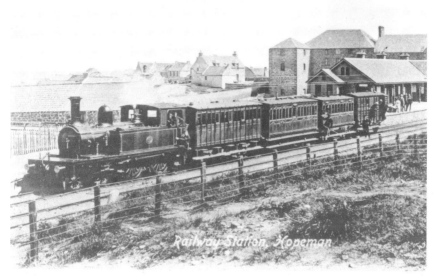

122 Hopeman station (HR) in Highland Railway days (LOS)

123 Hopeman station as caravan site headquarters, August 1986 (RRFK)

124   Burghead station (HR) in Highland Railway days looking towards
Hopeman (LOS)

125 Burghead station, August 1986 (RRFK)

126   Burghead station looking south, August 1986 (RRFK)